Ewa Szary-Matywiecka

Malvina,
or Spoken and Written Word in the Novel

Translated by Magdalena Ożarska

CHARLES UNIVERSITY
KAROLINUM PRESS 2022

NATIONAL PROGRAMME
FOR THE DEVELOPMENT OF HUMANITIES

Ewa Szary-Matywiecka is professor emerita at the Institute
for Literary Research of the Polish Academy of Sciences in Warsaw.

Magdalena Ożarska is associate professor of English
at Jan Kochanowski University in Kielce.

KAROLINUM PRESS
Karolinum Press is a publishing department of Charles University
Ovocný trh 560/5, 116 36 Prague 1, Czech Republic
www.karolinum.cz

English revision by Ursula Phillips
Cover by Jan Šerých
Graphic design by Zdeněk Ziegler
Illustrations on the cover and inside are from the 1822 edition
of Maria Wirtemberska's *Malwina czyli domyślność serca*, published
in Warsaw by N. Glucksberg. The images appear courtesy of Wikimedia.
Set and printed in the Czech Republic by Karolinum Press
First English edition

Cataloguing-in-Publication Data is available from the National Library
of the Czech Republic

The translation and publication of this book have been financed
by the Polish Ministry of Education and Science (Ministerstwo Edukacji
i Nauki) under the National Programme for the Development
of Humanities (Narodowy Program Rozwoju Humanistyki),
Grant No. 0205/NPRH4/H3a/83/2016.

ISBN 978-80-246-4532-2
ISBN 978-80-246-4520-9 (pdf)

Translator's Acknowledgements

The translator wishes to express her heartfelt gratitude to the following persons for their invaluable contribution to the translation of this book:

Dr Ursula Phillips for her generous and unswerving support as language consultant. Without her the book would not be as it is.

Ms Anna Łojek of the Interlibrary Loan Department of the Jan Kochanowski University Library for her infallible efficiency when it came to procuring the needed books and articles, sometimes verging on the miraculous.

Olga Baird and Professor Joanna Nowakowska-Ozdoba for their help with translations from Russian.

Dr. Corinne Fournier Kiss for her help with translations from French.

Without the support of the Jan Kochanowski University in Kielce and the Polish Ministry of Education and Science, this project would not have been possible.

Contents

Introduction

1.

The book that you are holding in your hand is devoted to one of the earliest and most beautiful Polish novels, *Malvina, or the Heart's Intuition* [*Malwina, czyli domyślność serca*] by Maria Wirtemberska. This novel, published in 1816, became an instant success, and continues to amaze readers today. This is thanks to its ingenious plot complications, achieved as a result of the protagonist's misidentification of two brothers – both are called Ludomir, but only one is her beloved. The novel thus contains traces of the ancient motif of twin brothers, separated at birth, and subsequently ignorant of each other's existence.

The way in which Wirtemberska draws on this motif is remarkable. Plot complications in *Malvina* are determined both literally and metaphorically by twinned phenomena: the twindom of the two Ludomirs, shrouded in mystery, as well as the essentially twinned personal coincidences and oppositions, in which all the characters become involved through their family relationships, affections and social activities. This is what constitutes the gist of these complications. Malvina is confused by the incarnation of the man whom she considers to be a single Ludomir in two strikingly different individuals. This undermines her inner faith in reciprocated feeling: a symbol of personal unity between two individuals. These two phenomena, in turn, are strictly connected with the theatricality of the drawing-room, which offers opportunities to play with the personal identities of its attendees, the novel's characters. Moreover, the reason for this type of plot development in *Malvina* is the "twinning" of the narrator's tale and the characters' letters: the simultaneous compatibility and opposition of these two narrative forms highlights the conflicts which arise between the characters' explicit and hidden actions. The narrator's tale correlates with spoken statements made by the characters which are heard by those around them. The letters, in turn, complement this tale with content which is merely implied. As a result, it is from the narrative tale that we learn about Malvina and Ludomir's meetings; it is from Malvina's letters that we learn how these meetings emotionally torment her.

It is therefore difficult to view the plot complications in *Malvina* other than through the lens of the "twinned" co-existence of these two narrative forms: the tale offers a peculiar type of narratorial utterance, while the characters' letters are ultimately written reports. This is particularly true when it comes to the issue of the interdependence and separateness of the creative acts fulfilled by the "twinned" authorial and narratorial incarnations of Maria Wirtemberska herself.

Such a reading of *Malvina* is not only innovative, but also deeply justified. Firstly, it enables a connection to be forged between the spoken and written narration of the novel and the problem to be solved by the protagonist, i.e. how is she to determine the "truthfulness" of the spoken and heard utterances, as opposed to that of the written and readable ones, when both are carriers of emotion? Secondly, it highlights a correspondence between the question of personal identity and the duality of events related to Malvina and the Ludomir brothers, as well as in the dual spoken and written narratives which report on these very same events. And, last but not least, this reading of *Malvina* enables us to perceive that the foundation of all these literally and metaphorically "twinned" events is the "twinned" energy of meaning, released both through the use of speech and through the use of writing. It is within this same sphere that the fate of Malvina's relationship with one Ludomir, and not two Ludomirs, will finally be determined. Similarly, it is within the same sphere, following the division of Wirtemberska herself into the narrator and the authorial persona, that the nature of *Malvina*'s narration ultimately takes shape.

The phenomena and problems which I outline at this point I hope will rekindle readers' interest in this work by Wirtemberska, so that more may be said about her text than simply labelling it "a sentimental novel". It is hard to imagine that readers will remain unmoved by her fine analysis of the dovetailing of personal identities and dualities, a primary feature of the relationship between the characters and their self-perceptions. This very analysis is a result of Wirtemberska's masterful drawing on the twin brothers motif, as well as on the ancient dual or androgynous doppelgänger symbolism associated with it. Exploring the correspondence between issues of personal identity and duality, as presented by Wirtemberska, poses few problems. This is because of the present-day interest in dialogic, or – broadly speaking – interactive human relationships. Paradoxically, issues related to individual personality are observable only with regard to another personality or other personalities. What makes it easier still is the fact that Wirtemberska's approach to such questions is underpinned (as is much of our contemporary reflection on this subject) by reflections on the nature of human communication through language, and – vice versa – on the nature of received utterances, viewed as tangible signs of the status of personal and personality-related human relations and self-perceptions. Implicated in all this are, as the particular contemporary equivalent of the phenomena depicted by Wirtemberska, the assumptions of the philosophy of dialogue formulated in the twentieth century for example by Martin Buber, Mikhail Bakhtin and Józef Tischner, as well as by the field of communication studies, a speciality of the twentieth century (including linguistics, the philosophy of language of J. L. Austin, and semiotics).

This coincidence is by no means accidental. All the characteristics of both spoken and written communications by the Ludomir brothers, which Wirtemberska uses to portray the instability experienced by Malvina of her beloved's individuality and personality, are contained within the realm of pre-romantic theories of language and studies of individual languages. This is the case with major aspects of the eponymous heroine's positive or negative perceptions of Ludomir's respective incarnations. Hence, the occurrence and – conversely, non-occurrence, of intonation and gestures in negotiating the nuanced shades of meaning in spoken communication. This is also the case with the marking of certain features – or absence thereof – in both spoken and written communications, with the organic unity of the message conveyed. Similar issues were raised by Rousseau and Herder, when debating the fundamental issue of differences in meaning between spoken and written utterances. Thus, by renewing today our interest in Wirtemberska's skilful application of the Ludomir twins' discourse to her construction of the novel's plot, we are in fact referring back to both historical reflection on the nature of language and to the distinctive features of individual languages. Such considerations have undoubtedly influenced not only modern theories and descriptions of language, but also theories operating in the fields of sociology and philosophy. Of invaluable help in forging links between the manner of expression of *Malvina*'s characters and contemporary theories of language has been, among other sources, Zofia Florczak's *Europejskie źródła teorii językowych w Polsce na przełomie XVIII i XIX wieku* [European Sources of Polish Theories of Language at the Turn of the Nineteenth Century]. I cannot emphasize this enough: this book has been my guide to exploring language theories of the past.

Clearly, Wirtemberska must have been well acquainted with both established and innovative trends in seventeenth- and eighteenth-century European reflection on language. This is suggested, primarily, by her masterly depiction of how Malvina is led on – in her personal experience – by distinctive features of other characters' utterances. This view is also supported by the fact that, in Wirtemberska's literary salon, conscious attention was frequently drawn directly both to the Polish language in general and to articulated speech in particular. Wirtemberska's salon heard recitations of poems and readings of prose texts. *Malvina* itself was read aloud there. Language and word games were organized, in addition to what we might call today a seminar in semantics, devoted – in the literal sense of the word – to defining the verbal subtleties of selected Polish synonyms. Much enjoyed in Wirtemberska's salon, these linguistic pastimes, playful but also – in their own way – scholarly, remained in keeping with a general intellectual tendency among contemporary aristocrats and townspeople, aimed at dissemination of the Polish language, enhancement of its use as well as devotion to its study. Established in 1800, the Warsaw Learned Society [Towarzystwo Warszawskie Przyjaciół Nauk] pursued these very goals. The publication of Samuel Linde's *Dictionary of the Polish Language* was supported by the society, while compilation of a *Dictionary of Polish Synonyms* was initiated. These activities took place during the first two decades following Poland's loss of independence: any such initiatives or endeavours, aimed at preserving the Polish language, were viewed as acts of patriotism. In my discussion of Wirtemberska's salon, the study carried out there of synonyms and the nature of the Warsaw Learned Society's activities, I draw on the conclusions of the study by Alina Aleksandrowicz, "'Błękitne soboty' Wirtemberskiej" [Wirtemberska's "Blue Saturdays"] as well as her book *Z kręgu Marii Wirtemberskiej. Antologia* [The Circle of Maria Wirtemberska: An Anthology] (this anthology discusses poetic texts and the dictionary of synonyms produced by Wirtemberska's salon). For researchers interested in *Malvina*, both of these studies are essential reading, as is Florczak's study of pre-romantic theories of language.

2.

The love relationship between Malvina and Ludomir has been viewed as sentimental, which is why the entire novel has also been labelled as such. However, it is important to realize that the love between Malvina and Ludomir transcends the sentimental model. It is such a complex phenomenon it may be regarded as heralding the romantic model. From beneath the typically sentimental excesses of sensibility and ornamentation, which sometimes characterize the progress of the heroine's affairs of the heart, there emerge her "lively" affections and awakenings, originating from the confrontation of her words with Ludomir's ambiguous utterances. The way in which Wirtemberska presents emotional experience, often marked by directness and liveliness, situates her novel – within the Polish cultural milieu – somewhere between Franciszek Karpiński's sentimental and Adam Mickiewicz's early romantic love lyrics. On the one hand, Wirtemberska departs from the sentimental love lyric, written in her circle by Ludwik Kropiński; on the other, she is a pioneer in transcending the "ceiling" of emotional experiences, around which later Polish sentimental romances, by Kropiński, Feliks Bernatowicz and Łucja Rautenstrauchowa, would revolve. Situating Wirtemberska's novelistic rendering of emotions somewhere between Karpiński's and Mickiewicz's lyrical poetry is by no means unfounded. In one of his two studies of *Malvina*, Budzyk claims that Polish sentimentalism developed primarily in poetry: "The Polish *Nouvelle Héloïse* is actually Karpiński" (1966a, 81). It is not then a mistake to situate Wirtemberska between Karpiński and Mickiewicz, particularly in view of the fact that *Malvina*, being a sentimental novel, is closer to Rousseau's treatise on language (*L'Essai sur l'origine des langues*) than it is to his *Nouvelle Héloïse*. Moreover, at the same time, *Malvina* has much in common with the spirit of Mickiewicz's *Sonnets*, published in 1826.

Just like Rousseau and Herder, Wirtemberska linked the phenomenon of love with the human capacity for verbal expression and communication through language. In her view, love does not happen in a void: it is supported by the implicit or explicit language acts of the person in love. In *Malvina*, she writes: "When one is very much in love, one's thoughts, soul, heart are occupied with this alone" (31).[1] It is in

---

1 All quotations from Maria Wirtemberska's novel are taken from *Malvina, or the Heart's Intuition*, translated with an introduction by Ursula Phillips, Northern Illinois UP, 2012. Hereafter, the novel's title will be generally abbreviated to *Malvina*, and references will be denoted by page numbers.

linguistic utterances that an individual's feelings and thoughts complement each other, as the other person becomes the object of his or her
affections. It does not matter whether these utterances are articulated in
one way or another, or merely expressed in thought. This is because in
both cases the linguistic utterance names the content of the feelings and
the content of the thoughts, thus effecting the complementation of these
elements. For Wirtemberska, linguistic utterances are precisely what enables the individual in love to render the emotion true and genuine. The
eponymous formula of "the heart's intuition", with which Wirtemberska
connects the name of her heroine, is the essence of the novel's presentation of love. It connects intuition, a particular intellectual endeavour,
which in the end dispels emotional doubts, with the heart – the symbol
of human emotional life.

Wirtemberska's simple truths would not matter to us or interest us
much were it not for the way in which she presents them in her novel:
in other words, if her novel did not show a heroine in the process of
solving a "real" dilemma of love. The heroine, who has to make a choice
between two personal representations of one beloved, is depicted both as
an individual who isolates herself from noisy human society and as one
who nonetheless connects with this very society. In consequence, there
appears an individual who experiences spoken utterances – both her own
and those of others – through the lens of the affective impulses of her own
inner monologue, traces of which are preserved in the letters which she
writes. Thus it emerges that what matters to us in Wirtemberska's view
on love lies in the transition from Karpiński's sentimental love lyrics to
Mickiewicz's early romantic love lyrics. At the same time, this very aspect
serves to separate her work from the sentimental salon lyrics of Ludwik Kropiński, Julian Ursyn Niemcewicz, Jan Maksymilian Fredro and
other authors. Teresa Kostkiewiczowa, an expert on Karpiński's poetry,
claims that in his most mature poems "the affairs of the heart between
two people" are presented from "an exclusively personal perspective":
"their significance, sense and charm are located precisely in the intimacy,
individuation, and subjective presentation of the experiencing subject"
(1964, 96–97). Through the use of symbols and allegory, the sentimental
lyric poetry of the salon portrayed the merits and works of love, but this
was done too generally to allow for the presentation of any individual
experience centred around particularised matters or events. In contrast,
what interests us most in Wirtemberska's project depends precisely on
the unveiling of particularised emotional experience, determined by both
personal and personality-related inclinations, as well as conditioned by

a particular environment. The experience manifests itself, for instance, in the emotional agitation of the body and the speech, ambiguous in meaning, but making it "genuine" precisely for this reason.

Wirtemberska's novel argues along the lines of Franciszek Karpiński's poem "Rozyno! Gdybyś wiedziała..." [Rosie-Anne, if you but knew...]: to begin with, love speaks not with words, but with the eyesight and with the touch. It is only later that true affection makes it possible for "soul with soul [to change] place": this affection cannot ultimately be translated into the language of the senses, or – for that matter – into the language of words:

Rosie-Anne, if you but knew
How love would set fire to
A couple of lovers childlike,
Childlike as your eyes look alike.

At the start came furtive
Glances, more than one, secretive,
The young lovers painstakingly
Disallowed their eyes to meet openly.

But when betrayed by confidence,
Meeting in a shared glance,
Both stare at the ground and hush,
With their cheeks a-blush.

Now each abandons the other,
Then come again together.
Both he and she withal
Burning with the sweetest fire of all.

Now their eyes grow bolder,
Now stand closer together,
And what their eyes revealed,
Their hands have duly sealed.

Their eyes send envoys fast
To their hearts of hearts;
Where other senses retreat,
Pure sensibility takes her seat.

The eyes fail; mute go the tongues:
Ardent love needs no sounds.
'Tis easy to say "I thee love"
When one has not loved enough.

The lovers their heads bend,
Put lip to lip, hand to hand,
In this tenderest embrace
Soul with soul changes place.

Can anything under heaven
Their sweet raptures even?
Ah, kings! Your glories and jewels bright
Seem nothing to such delight.
    (Karpiński 1960, 63–64; trans. M.O.)

At the same time, Wirtemberska's novel portrays the type of lover's maladjustment to reality that will become the preoccupation of Adam Mickiewicz's cycle of *Sonnets* ten years later. Moreover, in Wirtemberska's novel, the person in love experiences the same kind of communication-related pressures and the same kind of affective states of mind, which in the poems by Mickiewicz are signs of love-induced maladjustment. Below is one of these *Sonnets*, which may be quoted in support of this idea:

I talk to myself, with others am confused.
My heart throbs fast, beyond control my breath.
I feel sparks in my eyes, my face is blenched.
Some even ask aloud, how is my health,

Or, whispering, suspect I am deranged.
When thus fatigued I fall upon my bed,
Hope with a moment's sleep to ease my pain,
My heart sets blazing spectres in my head.

I leap up, run around and memorise
Words with which to curse your cruelty,
Memorise and forget a million times.

But when I see you, not a word will come.
Quiet again am I, colder than stone,
To burn anew – and as of old be dumb.
    (Sonnet II, Jones Debska 2012, 57)

The individual in love, as described in this poem escapes, just like Malvina, into spoken one-sidedness ("I talk to myself") and thus violates the rules of communicative reciprocity ("with others am confused"). In this emotional upheaval, the subject, just like Malvina, is driven by contradictory impulses (cursing and taking the curses back). In the end, semi-consciously, almost like Malvina, he surrenders to the need to experience the passion of love when appearances seem to testify to the beloved's absence: coldness and silence. In fact, there are only two differences in the ways Wirtemberska and Mickiewicz view the situation of an individual in love. One lies in gender: Wirtemberska's subject is female, while Mickiewicz's is male. The other difference is that in Mickiewicz's poem the loving subject becomes more enigmatic to others than Malvina does, and hence – more "isolated" than she.

In order to perceive and appreciate Wirtemberska's innovative approach to the novelistic presentation of emotions in the Polish literary culture of the early nineteenth century, it is not enough to contextualise them against the backdrop of contemporary popular romances by Madame de Genlis or Madame Cottin. It is necessary to consider the spiritual climate of this period of transition, sparked in Europe by Rousseau's and Herder's philosophies of emotion, as well as – where needed – the novelistic convention introduced by Laurence Sterne, which Wirtemberska herself indicated as her model. As it happens, Rousseau's and Herder's philosophies of feeling, which reflected the overall cultural shift from the Enlightenment to Romanticism, were both philosophies of language. Maria Renata Mayenowa, when outlining the main strands in the philosophies at issue, makes clear that "language was born out of the need for emotional expression. Emotion drew a scream from the lips of a primeval human being. More than that, this emotional origin serves to explain how sounds became its means of expression" (1970, 18; trans. M.O.). Let us remember that Rousseau, the philosopher of feeling, was the author of *L'Essai sur l'origine des langues* and *La Nouvelle Héloïse*, one of the first major models of the popular sentimental romance, whereas Herder's philosophy of feeling, as outlined in his "Treatise on the Origin of Language", coincides with Johann Wolfgang Goethe's *The Sorrows of Young Werther*, another major model of the popular sentimental romance.

Hence, if one wishes to properly appreciate and analyse Wirtemberska's achievement against the background of Polish literary culture, it is impossible not to relate the novel and the emotional life depicted in it to the spiritual climate of the epoch, which was focused on the direct proximity of three spheres of human behaviour: language, feeling and morality. Mere contextualisation of Wirtemberska's novel linking it to sentimental romances by Madame de Genlis or Madame Cottin will not do justice to the essence of her achievement, not to mention the significance of the linguistic initiatives and activities which originated in her salon. Wirtemberska's work has actually been juxtaposed with one particular work by Madame Cottin, who used the Ossianic name of Malvina in her title: initially, plot similarities were sought (see Kleiner 1981), and then – much more convincingly – parallels in both texts using the dual narrative forms of a tale and letters (see Budzyk 1966a). I do not mean to say that Cottin's novel played no part in the creation of *Malvina*. I do think, however, that it was not its main inspiration. This can be deduced from, I believe, a whole range of intellectual and literary impulses which simultaneously influenced *Malvina* and whose traces can easily be found in the novel. Here I mean the inspirations from Rousseau, Sterne, Ossian, Delille and others. My conviction concerning the literary genesis of *Malvina* owes much to the standpoint expressed by Witold Billip: "The sources of this remarkable text are to be located in almost everything which this violent epoch of forthcoming transition had to offer in terms of novel writing (this was the epoch which produced 12,000 volumes of romances in twenty-four years!): the English pre-romantic gothic romance, the Ossianic longing for the Middle Ages – the days of strong emotions and beautifully strong-minded knights, the passionate effusions of the miserable Saint Preux in *La Nouvelle Héloïse* or the desperate self-knowledge of Werther. *Malvina* would not have appeared without all of these literary inspirations, which were imported into Poland from France, England or Germany" (Billip 1978, 28; trans. M.O.).

3.

My book devoted to Wirtemberska's *Malvina* studies the novel's spoken and written narration. It covers two classes of problems. On the one hand, there are those resulting from the functioning of *Malvina* against the backdrop of the seventeenth- and eighteenth-century literary salon culture, in which speech and the written word enjoyed a comfortable co-existence. On the other hand, there are the issues related to the oscillation of the novel's narration between these two modes of utterance. The former associated with the salon-based readings aloud of *Malvina* are, to me, rather clear, while the latter require more careful discussion. The narration in *Malvina* relies on the dovetailing of the narrator's tale with the characters' letters. The tale, although inscribed both by the narrator and the author (I will clarify this in due course), has the status of a narratorial utterance. The characters' letters are, in contrast, unambiguously written documents. Both sets of issues, connected as they are with *Malvina's* spoken and written *narrations*, form the framework for this book, within which I also venture to ponder other equally significant, but more specific aspects.

One is *Malvina's* uniting of the narrative transitions from the tale to the letters (or vice versa) with the complexities of the plot. In order to examine this question, I focus on *Malvina*'s Warsaw episode. Characterised by a narrative speed fast enough to ensure that the "running" emplotment of events keeps up with both the tale and the letters in presenting the heroine's emotional dilemma, it offers a method for interpreting that dilemma. As with the tale and the letters.

Another central question I consider in order to define my research framework is the interweaving of the major elements in the Warsaw plot, that is the twin duality of Ludomir and the ambivalence of the personalities of the salon regulars, with a paired arrangement of characters who play their parts throughout the novel's entire plot: two sisters and two brothers. Focusing on this feature of the narrative, I analyse the parts played by the (literally and metaphorically) twin personal identities and dualities in the accumulating complexities of the novel's plot.

The third and last issue which I discuss is the presence of patterns of "twin" personal identity and duality, not only on the chronological plane, but also on the novel's narrative plane which presents them. These need to be considered on account of the interdependence, as well as separateness of the creative functions fulfilled by Wirtemberska's own "twin" incarnations: both as the novel's author and as the narrator who tells the tale of Malvina and quotes her letters.

While examining all these central and framework-related issues, around which my book is organised, I will continue to refer to two sets of phenomena, whose essence is the cross-reference between speech and writing. The first is *Malvina*'s interplay between similarities and differences in the nature and functioning of the tale and letters as narrative forms. The tale, which implicitly combines the properties of the written and spoken utterance, is associated with the conspicuous situation-based utterances of the characters spoken aloud, while the letters – as written communications – resonate with the characters' withdrawal from overt, verbalised, situational contact. The second set of phenomena, on the other hand, are the similarities and differences that Malvina observes between the quality of meaning in the spoken and written utterances made by the two personal incarnations of Ludomir. It is around these issues that my book revolves. Through the the first set of issues, the personal identity and simultaneous duality of Wirtemberska as author and as narrator is manifested. By means of the second set, the personal identity and duality of the main hero are manifested. Thus I am aiming in my book towards the following conclusion: in Wirtemberska's work, "twinned" meanings are linked doubly to speech and to writing, thus also pointing to (literally and metaphorically) "twinned" unities and dualities in personality. Likewise, conversely, these latter twin manifestations refer back to those related to the "twinned" qualities of speech and writing as bearers of meaning. Distinguishing speech and writing as the main preoccupations of my book on Wirtemberska is therefore the result of certain basic assumptions. The "twinned" semantic qualities of speech and writing, internally connected to each other, constitute in *Malvina* the essence of both its spoken and written narrations, as well as its plot which is centred on the motif of twin brothers. The phenomena of speech and writing are moreover the foundation for Wirtemberska's novel's functioning within the realm of the speech-and-writing culture of seventeenth- and eighteenth-century literary salons.

There are also further, equally fundamental, reasons that have made me focus on issues of speech and writing. When embarking on a discussion of the "twinned" correspondences of these phenomena in Wirtemberska's novel, we cannot help but discuss the problems associated with the narration of any novel, not just the one created by Wirtemberska. I would like readers to keep this in mind when reading my book.

Novelistic narration, even when not – as in the case of *Malvina* – so distinctly split into speech and writing, draws on the illusion of oscillation between the presented and the real properties of speech and writing. Novelistic narration is always created by a certain interplay between the properties of the presented utterance (by the narrator) and the properties of the real written word (by the author or the narrator-author). This interplay, manifest in novelistic narration, when viewed from the speech-and-writing perspective of *Malvina*'s narrative, would appear to be the interplay between the "twinned" interconnections between the properties of the presented spoken-aloud utterance and the real written word. We participate in this interplay both through the process of reading *Malvina* as we move from the tale sections to the letter sections (or vice versa), and through surrendering to the phenomenon of novelistic speech, like when we read the opening sentence, for example, of Witold Gombrowicz's *Cosmos*: "But let me tell you about another, even more curious adventure" (1985, 9). My objective in this book, apart from analysing *Malvina*, is to pinpoint and discuss the problems related to this "twinned", and hence illusive, nature of any novelistic narration which oscillates between the presented and the real properties of articulated speech and the written word.

4.

The methodological backdrop to my book on *Malvina* may be traced back to the development of structuralism in literary studies, from the pre-war beginnings of this school of thought, stretching back to Russian formalism, to its most recent intertextual incarnations. My study draws on a number of research procedures based on both past and contemporary structural understandings of literature. At this point, let me simply list those procedures which most broadly define my own approach. Like other structuralists, it is of crucial importance to me to focus on the properties of the links between the emerging ingredients of a literary work. I believe that understanding the "inside" of a literary work leads to understanding its meanings. I also believe that the knowledge thus obtained is the key to capturing the literary work's relatedness to tradition, whether in terms of genre or style, as well as its originality, such as its individual generic or stylistic expression.

I share the opinion of structuralist scholars, who have paved the way since the 1970s, that the constituent elements and factors which make up a literary work are textually heterogeneous. I also believe that they remain in complex relationships with one another, some of the relationships being simultaneous (parallel), but at the same time – ambivalent (dualistic) in terms of meaning. These convictions have enabled me to glimpse "inside" a literary work as the meeting space of a whole range of diverse "languages", "discourses" and "utterances". I also agree with Janusz Sławiński that today's rehabilitation of heterogeneity does not mean in the least that our discipline wishes to revert to the level of unlimited and unstructured research material, or abandon a well-defined concept of its own subject matter. Such a reversal would be, for one thing, impossible, because it would assume a return to former methodological unconsciousness under conditions not only of awakened, but also of heightened, awareness. The heterogeneity at issue here pertains indisputably to the subject and not to the material (the material is always heterogeneous). (1975, 51–52).

I am therefore assuming that investigation of the inner workings of a literary work, which leads to understanding of its meaning, is in fact identical to recreating the inter-text which constitutes it, within the confines of which these meanings reveal their significance.

The focus of intertextuality-related issues in my book is an examination of the properties of speech and writing in *Malvina*'s narration. These issues are linked to my objective of bringing to scholarly attention problems resulting from written expression in novelistic works, alongside my discussion of *Malvina*'s narrative features.

Since before World War II, Polish structuralists have been endeavouring in their study of the novel to outline the variety of narrative forms and utterance types used to present novelistic events. This boils down, in general terms, to a debate about the patterns that emerge from the various narrative and utterance-based constituents of a novel. The direction taken by Polish scholarship in this field has witnessed several studies on "narration", "characters' speech", "dialogue" and "direct speech presentation". A fundamental role in these studies has been played by the concept of "formal mimetism", developed by Michał Głowiński, as well by as the concept of personal relations developed by Aleksandra Okopień-Sławińska. The concept of formal mimetism revolves around the interplay between the novel and other types of literary utterance contained in it, such as the personal journal (Głowiński 1973c). Okopień-Sławińska's concept, in turn, revolves around observation of the complex relationships between diverse narrative and utterance-based forms. Okopień-Sławińska notes that these forms follow the nature of "personal relations." Some forms adapt to others as speech acts. The interconnections between them trigger an extremely complex network of relationships "whose centre is the sender-recipient I-you relation" (1985, 47; trans. M.O.).

My own research project, whose fruit is the present book on *Malvina*, is meant as a contribution to the discussion on the variety of narrative and utterance-based forms, as well as on the complexity of their interrelationships, investigated in the above-mentioned and other studies. My aim is to present these problems with reference to the written expression of novelistic works, and Wirtemberska's *Malvina* provides a useful model for a discussion of these very issues. To be sure, if it were not a novel which draws on the twin brother motif, that is, if it did not contain remnants of the ancient double androgyny and doppelgänger symbolism, it would not be able to "enter into the role" of example to illustrate these theoretical issues. And had it not done so, the nature of its narration and composition would not be as remarkable as it is.

Part One
In and Beyond the Salon

Wanda! Ludomir's voice, which has so much power over
my being, those precious tones, which I have not heard for
so many months, then took control of my senses, and at that
moment I forgot all Ludomir's faults and almost said
with the sincerity of my former attachment: "Ludomir, surely
people are blackening your name saying you no longer love
Malvina – *Malvina, who will never be able to forget you!*"[2]

Spoken Word, Written Word and the Novel

The letters of Maria Wirtemberska, as well as critical biographies and
studies of her literary work justify the view that her novel, *Malvina, or
the Heart's Intuition*, which the author herself labelled a romance, became
a connecting point for two different communicative situations soon after
it was first presented to the reading public.[3] In 1816 Wirtemberska's book
was published anonymously and reached wide circles of readers; Wirtemberska, however, wrote *Malvina* in 1812. In that same year the novel was

---

2 From *Malvina*, 57. In order to focus exclusively on the heroine's utterances, I am including in
   this footnote two statements, one of which might precede the motto, and the other – follow
   it. The former comes from J. G. Herder's 1772 "Treatise on the Origin of Language": "the
   sounds do not speak much, but they do so strongly" (2004, 66); the latter comes from Edward
   Sapir's 1949 "Speech as a Personality Trait": "the voice is to a large extent an unconscious
   symbolisation of one's general attitude" (1973, 537).
3 In the earliest editions of the novel, the characters' monologues and dialogues tend to be
   italicised and thus set off against the body of the narrative into which they are inserted.
   Contemporary Polish editions have liberated them from this textual narrative framework and
   subordinated them entirely to the discursive, dramatic logic of their paragraph arrangement in
   the novel. In this way, the transitory and evolutionary nature of these utterances is eliminated;
   they become narrativised, but it is clear that they remain monologues and dialogues.

probably revised by the poet and novelist Ludwik Kropiński, a regular of Wirtemberska's salon,[4] and since 1813 it had been read aloud in its author's salon to writers, literary critics and other literary connoisseurs. Before *Malvina* was ever received through reading, it circulated first in a theatrical mode – offering listeners a sensual experience through the dramatic reading aloud by Tadeusz Matuszewicz, a politician and orator.[5]

Surviving historical records can tell us little about the contemporary Warsaw salon convention of reading aloud literary texts, particularly prose, and the methods possibly used by the dramatic reader of *Malvina*. We have no way of knowing how his voice, or – to be precise – his intonation (in those days referred to as "the variations in tone"),[6] in combination with changes in his posture, gesticulation and facial expression, served to transform *Malvina* into a declamatory utterance, one to be listened to. However, the novel is neither explicitly rhetorical nor melodious. It is impossible to know how, if at all, the dramatic reader varied the sound of the two constituents of the novel, very different in terms of structure and narration, i.e. the narrator's tale and the characters' letters. What rhetorical and intonational principles were adopted? Did he follow the principle of "enchantment and pleasure", or perhaps that of the "inner significance of things"?[7] It is certain, however, that the suggestiveness of these readings inspired listeners to enter the roles of *Malvina's* characters by using acting techniques, and to start imitating their speech mannerisms and behaviours. In a nutshell, the circles influenced by Wirtemberska's salon began to use *Malvina* as an object of social interaction, as we would say today. This is how, in 1815, Wirtemberska herself commented on audience responses to the pre-publication dramatic presentation of *Malvina*, ranging from imitation to assimilation of the text:

---

4   For more information on the readings aloud of *Malvina* at Wirtemberska's salon, see: Duchińska 1886; Aleksandrowicz 1974, 1978; Billip 1978.

5   General information on Matuszewicz's acting and dramatic readings, along with their contemporary assessment, may be found in Jacek Lipiński's paper "Aktor i scena w recenzjach teatralnych Towarzystwa Iksów".

6   This term was used by Ludwik Osiński to mean the consciously modulated strength of the voice: "It is a mistake to believe that the higher the pitch we speak, the better we are heard. This would be to confuse the strength of one's chest with the pitch one selects. Without change to the pitch, we can strengthen or weaken the voice" (1862, 195; trans. M.O.).

7   This is another reference to Osiński, who reduces a whole range of poetry and prose reciting techniques to these two basic yet opposing categories (1862, 206–207).

Recently, at a ball at Mme Rzewuska's, Mme Aleksander Potocka, together with Strzyżewski and a young child, represented the family of Dżęga, because nothing can now happen without a reference to *Malvina*, which continues to be much in vogue. [...] All the townspeople adore it and want to have it translated into German. (Duchińska 1886, 32–33; trans. M.O.)

Although we have no details of the declamatory skills of *Malvina*'s dramatic reader, it may be assumed that it was not only he himself but the salon audience as well that – apart from the readings aloud from *Malvina* – re-enacted the novel in an active, externalised, almost theatrical manner. This was done not only through on-stage re-enactment of selected scenes from the novel, but also through modelling individual lifestyles on the novel's speech mannerisms, emotional responses, modes of action, etc. This is perhaps the real meaning of the above-quoted letter fragment: "nothing can now happen without a reference to *Malvina*, which continues to be much in vogue".

Malvina was preceded by a preface – a dedicatory letter from the author to her brother, Adam Jerzy Czartoryski. The presence of this letter-foreword demarcates the boundary between the closed and open modes of the work's existence and reception. It highlights the fact that the letter had no autonomy of its own and that it performed a merely auxiliary function with regard to *Malvina*'s existence in book form. This existence went beyond the salon, beyond the backstage of the writerly and theatrical worlds, and beyond the potential participation of the novel's recipients in the novel's actual composition (as was the case with Kropiński), i.e. beyond the possibilities for direct interaction between the novel's recipients and the novel's author. At the same time, it must be noted that the essence of this auxiliary function of the letter-foreword was (and still is) to lay the foundations, in circumstances where *Malvina* existed as a book, for a direct and text-based reference to its very source, to the act of writing, and to the figure of the novelist herself.

It would seem easier to reconstruct a range of reasons for reader satisfaction with *Malvina*'s publication in book form than to identify the declamatory conventions embraced by the dramatic reader and his salon audience. This kind of reconstruction lies beyond the scope of my book. Instead, I wish to draw attention to the merits of *Malvina* as a literary work, which can naturally be read aloud just as it was at Wirtemberska's salon. The novel, however, was originally designed by its author to be read, and not listened to. In addition, I intend to emphasise the most significant and most topical (in the eyes of its first critics) merits of *Malvi-*

na, the appreciation of which needs to be viewed as part of the general contemporary reception of the novel, acquired through a genuine reading experience. To illustrate these issues, I will draw, first of all, on a review by Jan Śniadecki, published anonymously. The review comes in the form of a letter from a father figure to a young, inexperienced person: an uncle writing to his niece, entitled "List stryja do synowicy, pisany z Warszawy 31 stycznia 1816 roku z przesłaniem nowego romansu" [An Uncle's Epistle to his Niece, Written from Warsaw on 31 January 1816, on Sending her a New Romance]. The letter writer, the uncle, recommends that his niece read *Malvina* – a romance, a text of the kind he had used to warn her against as "harmful and dangerous" (Śniadecki 2003, 22; trans. M.O.).

This review is central to issues related to writing, as well as to customs and manners, which Wirtemberska must have addressed while working on *Malvina. In* the dedication letter, attached to the novel and addressed "To My Brother", *they are* elevated to the *joint* sphere of ethics and poetics. Śniadecki's review explores these issues both through its rare, but carefully selected, form of an instructive epistle, and its exemplary argumentation demonstrating what it is that makes *Malvina's* "imaginary ways of the world" capture the imagination of readers (2003, 22; trans. M.O.). Śniadecki demonstrates that these "ways" do not pervert "youth's most crucial powers of imagination and sensibility" (2003, 22; trans. M.O.), as tends to be the case with other romances. On the contrary, the "imaginary ways of the world" enable readers to deduce "those rules of life which ought to guide the conduct of an exemplary, respectable woman" (Śniadecki 2003, 22; trans. M.O.).

In her dedication letter, Wirtemberska classifies her work as a romance. At the same time, she contrasts it with "romances written by [Ignacy] Krasicki, [Franciszek Salezy] Jezierski, and others" (3) on account of the differences in selection and arrangement of events between her novel and those belonging to the Enlightenment. What is more, the Enlightenment works depict the customs of past generations, of "our fathers and grandfathers", while *Malvina* portrays "our present-day society" (3).[8] At this point, it must be stressed that the entire content of

---

8   Maria Wirtemberska, *"To My Brother"*, in: *Malvina, or the Heart's Intuition* (3–4). The first to observe, appreciate and discuss the significance of this opposition was Kazimierz Budzyk (1966b). In his view, Wirtemberska's stress on *Malvina's* "present-day" aspects is all the more important because Ignacy Krasicki's tales, which she draws on as counter examples, are in their own way "also contemporary". From a didactic viewpoint, they forge a link between the past and the present. *Mr. Nicholas Wisdom* discusses topical issues, but does so through discovering the genealogy of the present day – the genealogy of the times with which, he assumes, his readers are familiar. *Malvina* does exactly the opposite. Its author is interested neither in

Wirtemberska's letter to her brother, including this statement of *Malvina*'s superiority over Krasicki's and Jezierski's texts, is permeated by the novelist's belief that all human endeavour ultimately fails to attain success, perfection and happiness. That is why Wirtemberska's assessment of *Malvina, her own work,* aspires to appear independent of her own, inevitably biased, opinion. Mindful of the lesson which the eighteenth century received from La Rochefoucauld, she begins her letter-foreword with these words: "I do not possess sufficient vanity to pretend to ascribe to You a work so lacking in excellence" (3). I believe that reading this confession, alongside the modesty topos which dominates Wirtemberska's epistolary foreword, as a mere dedicatory gesture does not do full justice to the novelist's intention. I believe, with Kazimierz Budzyk, that the foreword to *Malvina* "documents the writer's well-developed literary self-awareness" (1966b, 145; trans. M.O.). Following on from this, I aim at a holistic reading of the foreword rather than, as Budzyk seems to suggest, reading it as a set of distinct statements to be taken literally.

Wirtemberska's own assessment of her work cannot be read in isolation from the belief on which she elaborates, namely that the merit of any action lies in its very idea ("my own good intentions", 3), and not ultimate ("complete", 3) fulfilment. Whatever the author has to say in her foreword about *Malvina* as her own novel, about *Malvina* as a romance, and also about the romance as one of many "writing genres", oscillates between two ideas, both of which are important to her. These are: firstly, the conviction, which she does not formulate straightforwardly but merely implies, concerning the incomplete nature of any intention; and secondly, the openly expressed hope (a shadow of hope perhaps) to see her brother, "sacrificing [his] own life for the sake of others and for the universal good", "completely happy" (4).

Wirtemberska views her own work, and through this perspective also other texts of the romance genre, in the same way she views any imperfect human intention: as remarkable accomplishments. This is because romances, whose very essence is human-centred, are capable of suggesting to readers *representations* of those events, emotions, passions, and so on, in which they are personally involved in the world they inhabit. These are reflections of relationships between individuals, and between individuals and their own selves: relationships which are far from perfect,

---

a genealogy nor in a didactic anticipation of the present. In full consciousness of what she is doing, she sets out to capture what Krasicki completely misses: the present day for its own sake" (Budzyk 1966b, 146; trans. M.O.).

which abound with mistakes, and which may at times be reprehensible. Another belief of Wirtemberska's is that the romance itself, by offering opportunities to compare the readers' own faults and errors, committed in real life, with those invented by the writer, alerts them to moral actions ("virtue", 4) resulting from the necessary choice between "one" and "the other" ("a result of those reflections", 4), thereby helping to understand what moral actions are and what they result in (i.e. "happiness"). At this point in her argument, the stress which Wirtemberska puts on the "portrait of our present-day society" (3) presented in *Malvina* reveals its full significance not only in polemical but also structural terms. In the writer's view, the recipients' opportunity for a comparative overview of this portrait and their internalisation of it, may turn it into an ethical (rather than a merely instructive) inspiration. Here is Wirtemberska's impressive line of thought:

> Whereas in romances, in those faithful portraits of society, in which almost every reader encounters events similar to those he or she has experienced, emotions familiar to his own heart, errors into which he himself has fallen, passions which he has met often in life, that reader involuntarily becomes caught up in the portrayal, makes comparisons, reflects. And often as a result of those reflections, made without prejudice, the conviction takes root in his heart that whatever his fate, whatever his circumstances, striving for virtue is a more certain way than any other of striving for happiness. (3–4; italics original)

Focusing on the polemical objective of the foreword as a whole, aimed against the didactic novel of the Enlightenment, Kazimierz Budzyk claims that Wirtemberska meant to "reject the duty to immediately affect human actions", wishing instead "to shape human consciousness" (1966b, 148; trans. M.O.). This is when Śniadecki's argumentation in favour of *Malvina*, against the backdrop of his decidedly critical view of romances in general, begins to interact with Wirtemberska's argumentation aimed at the defence and appreciation of this genre.

Romance reading was, according to Budzyk, a "problem related to customs and manners" since the Enlightenment (1966b, 148; trans. M.O.). On the one hand, the popularity of the romance with readers clashed with negative views about this very popularity. Budzyk has demonstrated that some romances themselves contained explicit criticism of the genre, stigmatising its ludic goals, while those romances aimed at goals situated at the opposite end of the spectrum, i.e. didactic, catered to current social demand. This kind of criticism is found in Krasicki's two texts. On the other hand, stabilisation of the romance genre and the still growing interest of readers (irrespective of contemporary criticisms) were both conducive to the emergence of new varieties of the genre. These emerged out of resistance to didacticism, to date an inseparable part of the romance. This was clearly demonstrated by the appearance of *Malvina*. It is telling that Wirtemberska viewed the problem of the romance on two planes: with reference to the form which her novel had assumed, as discussed in the letter-foreword, and with reference to the female characters presented in the text, who follow "bookish" and "romance-based" ideas in their attitudes towards people, objects and events. In *Malvina*, the presentation of romance reading as a distinctive feature of contemporary customs and manners, which Budzyk barely mentions, replaces explicit criticism of this activity.

Agreement between Wirtemberska and Śniadecki on the subject of the romance genre is far from complete. There is also no complete concurrence between them as to what moral lesson or concept of personal happiness Niece Zosia [Sophie] ought to take from her reading of *Malvina*, despite all the merits of *Malvina* highlighted by Śniadecki.

From the range of possible methods used to instil the romance with "prescriptions, truths and lessons" (3), Wirtemberska accepts those which on the face of it do not rely on moral teachings, yet are capable of attracting readership. Wirtemberska believes that both the springboard to and foundation of didacticism in the romance ought to be located in its ability to entertain. Strictly speaking, this ability, with both its surface and deeper layers, is used as a pull factor. When readers engage with the surface layer (their active reading thus activated by "curiosity" and "feel[ing] inspired even to read", 3), their receptiveness to the deeper layer increases in proportion to how deeply they are involved in the former. The manner in which romances present moral teachings, unacceptable to Wirtemberska, is what she calls "dry moral precepts" (3), incapable of awakening in readers anything but indifference:

> It seems to me that the prescriptions, truths, lessons, which may be found in a romance beneath the mantle of entertainment, often do more to persuade than do dry moral precepts, stripped bare of the allurements that arouse curiosity and which few feel inspired even to read. (3)

In his review, Śniadecki raises several times the issue of Wirtemberska's fine gift of using "imaginary ways of the world", which helps direct readers onto the path that seems to him the most morally advisable and beneficial. Precisely from this follows his appreciation of Malvina's mode of kindling the readers' interest, neatly distributed and gradated across all the novel's constituents. This brings to mind the devices once used by Sterne, "whose chapter titles impress by their singularity but seem utterly disconnected, and yet they keep the secret and happy knot together, as well as maintaining the correct order of things" (Śniadecki 2003, 27; trans. M.O.). There is no doubt that Wirtemberska and Śniadecki concur in their opinion that the romance (but is this just about the romance, or perhaps about literature or art in general?) can only be justified if the text goes beyond the imaginary adventures of imaginary characters or situations invented simply to provoke pointless labours of "imagination and sensibility". These bear no fruit "in the real world". In a word, the romance ought not to limit itself to merely transporting readers into unreality, thereby reaffirming their spontaneous but narrow and naive views. It would seem, however, that beyond this point the ideas of the two writers about the romance in general and about Malvina in particular are no longer consistent. This pertains primarily to the issue of how the romance influences its readers as they discover its "prescriptions, truths, lessons" (3).

The argument presented in the letter-foreword demonstrates that Wirtemberska saw this influence as awakening her readers to ethical conduct in the real world and sensitising them to what may become the seed of an individual's conflict with the self or with other people in this world. She did not mean, even though she wrote approvingly of the "prescriptions, truths, lessons, which may be found in a romance beneath the mantle of entertainment" (3), to impose on her readers any concrete rules of conduct, presented through particular content and thus possible to internalise as didactic exhortations or commandments. Naturally, it could be said that one such imposable rule is contained in the already discussed "striving for virtue [being] a more certain way than any other of striving for happiness" (4). It is nonetheless so general that it fails to specify the kind of virtue or meaning of the happiness thus achieved, stressing only their co-dependence and significance for an individual fate. Moreover, it treats the "state of affairs" typical of virtue and happiness as a non-existent "state", one that belongs with the future, barely feasible. In consequence, the statement might be understood in another way. It is not a maxim formulated with a view to teaching individuals whose "tastes and inclinations", in need of being corrected along certain lines, are already known to the moralist. The addressee here is every reader of *Malvina*, "regardless of their tastes and inclinations".[9] This is not a piece of moralising but of ethical teaching: one that pertains to ethics, to be precise.

Śniadecki, unlike Wirtemberska, assumes the role of teacher and moralist with respect to readers of romances, and in particular to readers of *Malvina*. This explains why his remarks are in the first place addressed to his niece, Zosia.[10] His whole argument serves to emphasise the specification, clarification and explicit verbalisation of the moral wisdom which he reads into *Malvina*. This is visible in the very form of the instructive epistle which he chooses for his argument, notwithstanding his conspicuous admiration for *Malvina*, appreciation of the novel's close-knit relationship between the interest-arousing "course of events, properly entangled" (Śniadecki 2003, 27; trans. M.O.), and its elevated message. He recommends *Malvina*'s moral wisdom to his niece's attention as a set of guidelines which she may find helpful in order to correctly interpret the events presented in *the novel*. In this way, he hopes to reinforce the young lady's compliance with and respect for those moral values and principles which she might possibly be tempted to defy if misled by other romances. The final part of Śniadecki's epistolary review, following a summary of the plot of *Malvina*, enumerates the most important lessons found in the novel and contains this statement:

> I have summarised this book for you in order to satisfy your curiosity, too keen on knowing the ending, and to awaken your attention to exploring many a serious thought, to pondering many a danger into which unrestrained sensibility may throw us, and to collecting admonitions which may prove salutary to you. (Śniadecki 2003, 32; trans. M.O.)

If we look at the moral teachings contained in Śniadecki's epistolary review from the standpoint of the letter-foreword to *Malvina*, it becomes clear that these are not so far removed from the poetics of "dry moral precepts". It is difficult to correlate the following conclusion of Śniadecki's with Wirtemberska's thoughts on happiness as formulated

---

9   Here I refer to Ludwig Wittgenstein's notion of "absolute good, if it is a describable state of affairs, [...] one which everybody, independent of his tastes and inclinations, would *necessarily* bring about." This definition of "absolute good" is preceded by the following general remark: "Our words used as we use them in science, are vessels capable only of containing and conveying meaning and sense, natural meaning and sense. Ethics, if it is anything, is supernatural and our words will only express facts" (1993, 40).

10 It would seem that Śniadecki's didactic goal is also shown in his selection of the addressee's first name, Zosia [Sophie], very popular at the time.

in her foreword, or with the fulfilment of her protagonist's happiness as depicted in the novel – happiness that is equally threatened by untoward external circumstances and by the cognitive confusion which is partly her own fault:

> Yes, my dear Sophie! True and lasting happiness is almost never occasioned by a transitory fever of the heart, but by gentle stirrings which come from one's common sense and are reinforced by one's experience. (Śniadecki 2003, 33; trans. M.O.)

Naturally, it is not that the virtues of common sense and experience, those two forces which cool the heart, play no part in the protagonist's attainment of personal happiness. But they do not play the only role in this complex process, either. To achieve personal happiness, Malvina is required to demonstrate not only her common sense, manifested in her cautious and distanced attitude towards Prince Melsztyński, but also her self-loyalty, i.e. continuing to seek reasons to fuel her "fever'd heart" (Śniadecki 2003, 33). I hope I am not mistaken in suggesting that Wirtemberska and Śniadecki endorse two different concepts of happiness. I will return to this issue later in this book.

Everything that enabled Wirtemberska to underpin her own romance writing with her own theory of the genre may be linked to her view of poetics as being inseparable from ethical issues. This is what made her stance on the moral content of romances different from Śniadecki's views on *Malvina*'s moral message, which he narrowed down to a set of guidelines linked to respect for parental and marital values, and his model of the "exemplary, respectable woman" (Śniadecki 2003, 23).

The novelty of such an approach rested on Wirtemberska's intention to introduce romance readers not to moral teachings as such (in the form of "dry moral precepts"), but to the field of ethics, which extended in the real world beyond the romance. Wirtemberska never specified the morphological constituents of the romance, to which she ascribed the possibility of ethical influence on the readers. Based on the indirect characteristics of these constituents, it may be surmised that in fact she meant what is called today the novel's presented world, and more precisely, the event-related, emotional and moral resonance of that world which might then serve as a source of moral reflection to readers, and facilitate their understanding of their own passions, emotions and errors. In addition, it should be said, based both on previous assumptions and on our current knowledge of the novel genre, that this quality of the presented world both in the former romances and in today's novels has been achieved thanks to the suggestiveness produced by the combination of two morphological constituents: characters (i.e. representations of human beings) and plot (representations of characters' actions). Contemporary experts in the terminology shared by classical ethics and poetics stress the fundamental unity between the categories of *praxis* (action) and *ethos* (character), and that at its most profound it concerns the attainment of happiness. Paul Ricoeur agrees with James M. Redfield on this subject:

> Ethics, in effect, deals with happiness in its potential form. It considers its conditions, the virtues. But the connection between these virtues and the circumstances of happiness remains dependent upon contingencies. In constructing their plots, poets give intelligibility to this contingent connection. (1984, I: 241)

We may therefore assume that, in Wirtemberska's opinion, the social impact of the romance lay in the very combination of characters and action. More specifically, this is what the above researchers would call the ethical intelligibility of this combination.[11] Wirtemberska openly endorses the view that if the romance had any influence whatsoever, if it could teach its readers anything, then this goal was to be achieved by means far subtler than conspicuous didacticism. She considered the readers' curiosity to be a prerequisite to understanding, and the readers' indifference to be a prerequisite to misunderstanding.

Today we tend to classify *Malvina* not as a romance but as a novel. We consider it one of the first Polish realisations of the genre. Whether we are dealing here with a terminological or genric difference is an open question. Stanisław Burkot and Alina Witkowska maintain that contemporary Polish writers, when applying the label of romance to their works, remained in keeping with the then habit of referring to narrative prose works whose plots centred on love and adventure, as romances (Burkot 1968; Witkowska 1971). The term "novel" was still associated with "fantasy and fabulation full of improbable ideas and events" (Witkowska 1971, xv; trans. M.O.). Yet, in the European context, a variety of terms to denote the novel genre were in use, which is why it is difficult to accept the fact that terminological differences boil down to the mere

---

11   J. M. Redfield, in his discussion of the two Greek notions expressing two aspects of fame: *kudos* (originating from the grace of the gods, and immediate) and *kleos* ([passed on] from mouth to mouth, from generation to generation), notes that "[s]torytelling thus rises directly from the need for ethical intelligibility" (1994, 65).

giving of new names to the same phenomenon. This conviction of mine is supported by what Ian Watt says in *The Rise of the Novel*:

> Dr. Johnson, with the *novella* in mind, defined a "novel" as a "small tale, generally of love". When *Pamela* appeared it was called a "dilated novel", because its subject was essentially the single amorous episode which previous short novels had usually been concerned with, but its treatment was on a scale much closer to that of a romance. (1965, 164–165)

Hence it may make sense to assume, with caution, that regardless of the natural transition from the term "romance" to the term "novel" in Polish literary culture, in European culture it was accompanied by a wealth of evolutionary and transformative phenomena. These phenomena, jointly, may have contributed to the emergence of narrative forms which fulfilled the requirements that, customarily and generally, were beginning to be linked with the genre of the novel in nineteenth-century Europe, including Poland.

Spoken and Written Word in the Novel

By opening my discussion of *Malvina* with a description of the separate although successive communicative events, which it inspired and shaped, I intend to achieve two complementary goals. First, I wish to consider the distinction between *Malvina*'s "circulation" and its subsequent reception. The reception of this novel occurred either via the voice of a reader-interpreter, or in contrast via the text itself in book form. Let me stress once again that this reception coincided with the novel's transcending of its author's salon, its entry into another literary milieu and its reaching the widest possible audiences of the day, partly or wholly competent when it came to reading literature. Here are the questions concerning the two circulations and receptions of *Malvina* that interest me most: What were the differences between them? What fuelled them and what reduced them? How did these differences reveal themselves in the various uses made of *Malvina*'s verbal and semantic material by listeners in Wirtemberska's salon and readers outside the salon? To what extent did the differences between dramatic readings aloud of *Malvina* and individual readings of the book, i.e. between listening to *Malvina* being read aloud and the actual private reading of *Malvina* as a book to oneself, reveal incompatible communicative qualities? What constituted the essence of these qualities? Did it come only from the input into the communicative functioning of *Malvina*'s meaning from its "live" presentation and interpretation, achieved by means of a ringing, pulsating voice which disappeared into the listeners' ears? Or did it come from the silent mode of reception, intended for the readers' eyes only, relying on the formal arrangement and division of the verbal and semantic material of the book? Or perhaps the communicative qualities brought to life by the functional, expressive and symbolic oppositions between the words of *Malvina* enriched by the sound of a reader's voice and meant to be heard, and the same words read silently on one's own, were accompanied by other derivative constituents of meaning?

In addition, I wish to consider another problem: did the differences which informed and disconnected from one another the novel's two different reception modes, i.e. the listening and the reading, correspond at all to any phenomena within *Malvina* itself? This is the central question of this study. I am inclined to believe that the co-existence of the spoken and written narrative forms (the tale and the letters) in *Malvina* triggered types of communicative disconnections and co-dependencies parallel to those brought to life by the first public presentations of *Malvina*. In both cases, the similarities and differences between possible receptions and interpretations via the voice and via the eyes of the novel's recipients, would have been instrumental.

As I formulate this argument, I have in mind the spoken and written duality of *Malvina*'s narration. This is not an obvious feature. It can only appear within the novel's written mode, just like the already discussed dramatic readings aloud of the novel can appear only in the literary salon. The spoken and written narrative duality of *Malvina* arises from the efforts and actions of a "character", who – when presenting the events – either recounts them or includes letters written about them by participants in these events. And although this "character" repeatedly refers to herself not only as the narrator, but also as the novelist, her actions centre on the telling of the tale and the including of the letters. Since it is the tale which she tells and the letters which she includes that make up the novel's narrative units, and not her statements in which she represents herself as the novelist. These statements play a protective role with regard to the tale which she tells and the letters which she includes by situating them within the illusive framework of a novel. This protective role parallels the equally protective role played with regard to the tale and the letters by the author's real novel-writing acts.

The events presented in *Malvina* result, in their entirety, from this dual mode of their relating. They occur once in the tale – via the narrator's discourse, even though the latter is part of both the illusive and real novel-writing acts of the author. Then they occur again in the letters which are inserted into the narrator's tale. I shall centre my analysis of *Malvina*, firstly, on this narrative duality with its shifts between the acts of telling and of inclusion of written documents.[12] Secondly, my attention will focus on the thereby created co-dependence of these contrasting constituents of the narrative, i.e. the tale and the letters, in the presentation of events. Last but not least, I will discuss the already outlined "relationship" between the phenomena related to the readings aloud of *Malvina*, which reached the ears of listeners in the salon, and those which resulted from the novel's spoken and written narrative.

Within the novel genre, the tale and the letter had both been used for centuries. For a discussion of their presence in *Malvina*, however, more important are the more recent, i.e. seventeenth- and eighteenth-century stages of this tradition. It was during these centuries that two distinctive, contrasting types of the novel emerged, each separately reaching its apogee. Paul Ricoeur, in summarising the many publications on the novel of this period, labelled one of these types, as practised by Daniel

---

12 In order to offer a detailed discussion of *Malvina's* dual spoken and written narratives, by focusing my attention on formulas which remain in striking opposition, I wish to stress that we are dealing here with devices used for recounting extremely different events, ones which complement each other yet remain at the same time separate and even contradictory. The tale, after all, refers to the external "world" in which the events occur; the letters are its internal equivalent. I agree with Gérard Genette that, as readers and as researchers in the novel genre, we do not attach enough importance to the perfect dovetailing of these devices, or perhaps we should say – acts serving to represent (mimetic) events, which remain completely dissimilar in their profoundest essence. In his "Frontiers of Narrative", Genette aims to "point out the profoundly heterogeneous character of a mode of expression to which we are so used that we do not perceive its most sudden changes of register. Plato's 'mixed' narrative, that is to say, the most common and universal mode or relation, 'imitates' alternatively and in the same register ('without even seeing the difference,' as Michaux would say), non-verbal material, which in fact it must represent as best it can, and verbal material that represents itself, and which it is usually content to quote" (1982a, 131). I repeat this opinion of Genette's despite the fact that, as readers and researchers in the novel genre, thanks to the works of Michał Głowiński on formal mimetism, we have been sensitised to the typical, pervasive "tension or even interplay between various utterance types, for example between the novel and the personal journal to which the former refers" (1973c, 64; trans. M.O.). It would seem that for the analysis which I intend to conduct here, aimed as it is at demonstrating the alternation between the tale and the letters in the presentation of events, both the above representations of novelistic *mimesis* ought to be considered. One focuses on the internal conditioning of the production of *mimesis*, while the other – highlights the necessary external conditions.

Defoe, the pseudo-autobiographical novel. The other, as practised by Samuel Richardson, came to be known as the epistolary novel. Both terms remain in keeping with the time-honoured terminology used in studies on the novel genre.

Ricoeur's argument, as well as the studies from which he quotes, demonstrate that the failures of the former type of novel with regard to verisimilitude in the presentation of reality were compensated for by the latter. The pseudo-autobiographical novel met readers' expectations by presenting "the hero [who] recounted something after the fact", while the other featured "the hero [who] recounted something [...] directly from the scene" (1985, II: 12). A change in the understanding of novel-istic verisimilitude came about when a maximum proximity was intro-duced between characters' feelings and their acts of producing written discourse on the subject of these feelings. In pseudo-autobiographical novels, these acts take the form of memoirs; in epistolary novels – the form of letters. "By having his heroine immediately write things down, the novelist could convey the impression of great closeness between writing and feeling" (Ricoeur 1985, II: 11). Not only was the memory of one's experience conducive to the spinning of memoir-like tales, the im-mediacy of experience, which sprang from the epistolary records, helped convey an essential sense of verisimilitude to readers. Ricoeur tells us:

> The epistolary genre presupposes, in fact, that it is possible to transfer through writing, with no loss of persuasive power, the force of representation attached to the living voice or theatrical action. (1985, II: 12)

Ricoeur believes that the adjustment of both novel types to the requi-rements of verisimilitude, the former relying on modes of presentation that create the illusion of the infallibility of memory, and the latter – of sincerity of feeling, found an analogy in John Locke's views on language. In the late seventeenth century, these views gave way to other linguistic theories which were to proliferate in the eighteenth century. Ricoeur tells us that, for Locke, referentiality was the primary property of language, while imagery and ornamentation were secondary. Ricoeur thus conclu-des his discussion of the epistolary novel:

> To the belief, expressed by Locke, in the direct referential value of language stripped of ornaments and figures is added the belief in the authority of the printed word substituted for the absence of the living voice. (1985, II: 12)

Ricoeur's reasoning strengthens my belief that, by seeking to emphasise the correspondences between the listening and reading reception
modes of *Malvina* as well as its dual spoken and written narrative, I am
entering the realm of influences that shaped the European and Polish
novel at the turn of the eighteenth century. It would seem that, particularly in the light of the conclusions formulated directly by Ricoeur, and
indirectly by Ian Watt upon whom the former draws, that two categories
of factors were significant at this stage of the novel's development. On the
one hand, the printed form of the novel accentuates its secondary mode
of reference, as we might say today, one which creates its own system of
signs and meanings: a literary utterance. On the other hand, it imitates
the natural forms of speech and writing, from which the literary utterance
has become completely disconnected. It seems evident that the tradition
closest to the production of *Malvina* is the culture of French and Polish
literary salons. There is similarly no doubt that between the novels discussed by Ricoeur and *Malvina*, there had appeared prominent figures
such as Jean Jacques Rousseau and Laurence Sterne. Consequently, when
describing the spoken and written duality of *Malvina*'s reception and
narration, we are looking towards a fragment of a later stage in the development of the novel, as outlined by Ricoeur. This stage is not marked
by the names of Defoe and Richardson, but by those of Rousseau and
Sterne; and – which is equally important – it is affected by theories of
language, all of which grew out of Locke's thought, but accentuated at
the same time the significance of the imagery-related, figurative properties of language, which Locke himself had underestimated.[13]

For understandable reasons, at this point, I am not able to elaborate
on these historical and theoretical issues, because this would amount to
a discussion now of what will be explored in the following sections of this
study. I am assuming nevertheless that the spoken and written narrative
of *Malvina* contains two issues that may be investigated by scholars researching the novel genre. One concerns the literary, novelistic, bookish
tale. In order to place it at the centre of the presentation of events, and,
what is more, to raise it to the rank of a specific "presented reality", its
imitation of the written utterance will at times approximate to a spoken
utterance, and at other times distance itself from it. Simultaneously, its
fundamental task is to reflect speech acts: spoken-aloud, audible and
situation-based. The letters pose another problem: inserted into the tale,

---

13 Locke's impact on eighteenth-century theories of language and the theories themselves are
    discussed by Zofia Florczak (1978).

they contribute to the presentation of the events which the tale recounts, hence – to its reflection of speech acts. Yet, due to their structure of purely written communications, they act as devices by which distance from the meanings carried by the spoken-aloud, audible and situation-based utterances may be achieved.[14]

Another assumption I am making is that the essence of interdependence between the tale and the letters in *Malvina*, and the essence of the spoken-aloud and silent interpretation of *Malvina*, on which the dramatic and readerly modes of its early reception depended, lies in the relation of the novel to the sound – the most significant property of live speech, in material and symbolic terms. It is a fact that live speech, when deprived of sound, simply ceases to be. If this view is applied to *Malvina*, it becomes clear that the letters enable a certain liberation from the meanings of spoken utterances, communicated through this cardinal feature: the sound. This very liberation contributes to the novel's plot complications and structure. If this line of reasoning is used to consider the dramatic and readerly modes of *Malvina's* reception, it is impossible to miss the shifts from the audible to the visual, which, according to Gérard Genette, have accompanied over centuries of literary history the development of the mode of "silent diction" (1982b, 97) on the one hand, as opposed to what may be called "writerly, written texts", on the other:

---

14 By choosing to focus, in my discussion of *Malvina*, on the theoretical importance of analysing the imagery in the novelistic tale of spoken (audible) and written (silent) communications, I am following the path trodden by Polish researchers since the time of the pre-WW2 phenomenological and structuralist turn in literary studies. This turn and its consequences led to exploring the genric variations in narrative forms and characters' utterances which serve to present events in the novels. This boils down to the study of principles of communication and the hundreds of ways in which various narrative and utterance-based elements of a novel are connected. On the quality of these connections rest the representational and communicative properties of the novels. This has been the direction taken by studies on narrative, characters' speech, indirect speech and dialogue since before WW2 (cf. Budzyk 1946; Hopensztand 1946; Głowiński 1963; Górny 1966; Głowiński 1973). Michał Głowiński's concept of formal mimetism also belongs to this trend. Later, these research interests shifted towards the complex connections between varied narrative and utterance-based forms. It was observed, for instance, that their nature corresponds to that of personal relations. Some forms were found to adapt to others as speech acts. Their interconnections trigger a complex network of relations "whose centre is the sender-recipient I-you relation" (Okopień-Sławińska 1985, 47; trans. M.O.). This concept of personal relations was later developed into a theory of "sender-recipient set-ups inscribed into narrative texts" (Bartoszyński 1985, 113; trans. M.O.). I view my own research as a contribution to the discussion begun in these studies. My aim is to do so through the perspective of the spoken and written variation of narrative and utterance-based forms in literary texts (*Malvina* serves as a model), and at the same time – in connection with the written expression of these texts.

This change of criterion does not signify, however, that the phonic, rhythmic, metrical reality of ancient poetry is entirely lost (which would be a great pity); it has rather been transposed into the visual and, by that very fact, in some sense idealized; there is a silent way of perceiving "sound" effects, a sort of silent diction, similar to the experience of a musician reading a score. (Genette 1982b, 97)

Yet, in order to make the argument about the existence of analogous "structures" in *Malvina* and its reception truly convincing, the spoken and written duality of the novel's narrative should be viewed not only as a principle of composition; it also needs to be seen as a factor contributing both to the internal connections between the presented events, and to symbols generated by these connections. This approach to *Malvina's* spoken and written narrative may once again be supported by Ricoeur's conclusions. Having analysed Aristotle's *Poetics*, Ricoeur offers the following understanding of the essence of the actualization of events, on which literature, and the novel in particular, feeds:

The kind of universality that a plot calls for derives from its ordering, which brings about its completeness and its wholeness. The universals a plot engenders are not Platonic ideas. They are universals related to practical wisdom, hence to ethics and politics. A plot engenders such universals when the structure of its action rests on the connections internal to the action and not on external accidents. These internal connections as such are the beginning of the universalization. [...] To make up a plot is already to make the intelligible spring from the accidental, the universal from the singular, the necessary or the probable from the episodic. (Ricoeur 1984, I: 41)

The spoken and written modes of *Malvina's* narrative determine first and foremost the many turns of the plot: from explicit situations and milieus (constructed by and featured in the tale) to the characters' hidden thoughts and utterances (constructed by and featured in the inserted letters). These turns may be irregular or obscure, as they do not always correspond to the overarching division of the narrative and plot into chapters. They generate event-related tensions between the revealed and the concealed "planes" of characters' lives: those accessible to the characters' sight and hearing versus those accessible only to the eyes of the letters' addressees, hidden or possibly secret, and hence purposefully blurred. This duality of the spoken and written narrative is paralleled by the two planes of the characters' motivations and utterances. Their overt meanings, whether related to situations or milieus, are not the same as the meanings located on the hidden plane: within the characters' inner experiences and confessions contained in their letters. This two-plane structure of the characters' conduct and the latters' failure to express themselves freely grows increasingly important as Malvina comes to perceive Ludomir as a puzzling human being.

The symbolic aspect of the spoken and written duality of *Malvina*'s narration lies in the subordination of the main characters' actions to the conflicting factors of openness and secrecy. This is a cognitive contradiction of a much less tangible communicative nature than the contradiction between spoken and written communication. It is the contradiction which Malvina is beginning to face internally as she is confronted with circumstances that defy comprehension and engage equally her openness to the outside world (both human and natural) and her self-absorption, i.e. her sensibility and rational faculties, her heart and mind.

In conclusion, it may be said that the symbolic plot-related effects of the spoken and written duality of *Malvina*'s narrative transform the riddle into a mystery, which surfaces in connection with the character of Ludomir. Malvina's attempts to solve the mystery provide her with inner experiences in which reasoning combines with emotions. Who is Ludomir? How deep can the contradictions in the personal identity of one and the same individual reach? How to pinpoint this contradictory identity when it affects utterances, beliefs and emotions?

The Novelistic Tale: Written Word as Representation of Spoken Word

"Now the storm's over it feels so close indoors. We'd do well to open the verandah window."

"But, sister, the light will attract thousands of mosquitos!"

"The shutter won't let in the mosquitos, but the cool will reach us along with the sweet scent of the mignonette, which the rain must have refreshed. But it's not so much the mosquitos that you fear, my little coward," continued Malvina, smiling at her sister, "as the claps of thunder. Though it's true they have been quite powerful for the past few hours. But now they've completely died down, you should calm down too, my dear Wanda. And to make it easier for you to forget your fear, I shall play you that mazurka which you keep telling me makes you think of the most tantalising balls". (8)

Wirtemberska's *Malvina*, just like Sterne's *Sentimental Journey*, does not start with a tale but with a dialogue as the mode of novelistic utterance. That is why in *Malvina*, the beginning of the tale as exposition of the plot does not coincide with the beginning of the action. The time and place of the start of the action are indicated in the preceding dialogue between the two sisters, Malvina and Wanda. They talk about the thunderstorm and stuffy atmosphere, about mosquitos and prospects for cooler weather. Their dialogic exchange follows a pattern of affirmative statements and responses, repeated twice. The familiarity which predominates during the first part of the exchange gives way in the second to irony, which only corroborates the already indicated difference of opinion between the two characters, now additionally serving to underscore their different personalities. It is the appearance of this difference and discrepancy that becomes the starting point for the tale. As a supplement to Malvina's words, it steals into her utterance in order to supply the information about her "smile" and thus intensify the accompanying irony: "continued Malvina, smiling at her sister" (8). From now on, the tale directs the readers' attention towards the contrasts between Wanda's inner distractedness and Malvina's inner concentration; between the common sense of one sister's experience and the inspired nature of the other's. What matters in the opening scene is that Wanda only speaks, whereas Malvina both speaks and sings. What also matters is that Wanda shows herself to be insensitive to the "aesthetics" of darkness, while Malvina allows this darkness to permeate her thoughts. The open window, the thunder and lightning, the incoming mosquitos, the scent of the mignonette, a stir of unknown provenance which brings to mind the sound of footsteps, the open verandah window: all these things link the natural world with Malvina's affective mental states.

The tale spun by the female narrator, as she ponders the nature of and prerequisites for happiness in connection with the presented events, and comments on a variety of nuances in her own actions related to the presentation of these events, is set in the alternating milieus of an aristocratic manor house, and the salons and public-civic stage of Warsaw. It focuses on the generationally complicated circumstances in which the love of Malvina and Ludomir is eventually fulfilled in marriage, despite the obstacles. The tale itself, the letters excluded, only serves to inform the reader selectively about the progress of the protagonists' love relationship, and the bad effects of Ludomir's mysterious disappearance and subsequent reappearance following his negative transformation. This information is conveyed in a way that parallels the spontaneous growth of affection between Malvina and Ludomir: the affection is disclosed by them in spoken-aloud utterances, heard by third persons, as well as in actions and reactions which accompany these utterances or result from them. These behaviours are, according to the tale, subjected by them to "judgement" (Wirtemberska 2012, 13), or – as we would say today – situationally objectified (cf. quotation below). They are affected by both characters' observance of spoken conventions of secrecy, or even intentional concealment of emotion, likewise apparent in their suppression of their initial interest in each other, and their later emotional reciprocity, as well as in their following the conventional rules of polite behaviour.

The passage below shows how, for the first time in a conversation between Ludomir and Malvina (the tale follows the course of the conversation), as a result of the heroine's emotional agitation and faltering attention, they both become so self-absorbed and so focused on the words they utter that the conventional etiquette of dialogue is broken, and how, thanks to the hero's self-control and eloquence, its rules are promptly re-established:

> "My name is Ludomir. I was passing this way on my travels and had stopped at the post-house because of the storm. Taking advantage of a lull, I allowed myself to stray a while along the beautiful paths which led to a house whose owner [...] I can now readily imagine must be..."
>
> "Ah, and I too can now imagine, who [...] interrupted my singing this evening," Malvina was about to add. These words, about to escape from her lips, ran ahead of any judgement she might have exercised regarding their necessity; she blushed and did not finish her sentence, while Ludomir, observing her confusion, pretended he had not noticed and began to speak again:
>
> "When the tempest blew up a second time, I sheltered under a balcony not far from here. I heard the thunderbolt strike and soon noticed the fire. I then came running over and shall henceforth regard the hour when I could be of service to kindness and innocence, as the happiest of my life".
>
> Ludomir fell silent (13).

Malvina's immediate response to the message contained in Ludomir's words, originating in her repetition of his words, her abrupt breaking off in the middle of a sentence and his eloquent taking up of the conversation from that very point all demonstrate that their close, sensually charged presence and spoken utterances create an environment in which affective stimuli, experienced by both of them, can arise most naturally. It also shows how the process lapses into its opposite, and tends towards conscious concealment of the protagonists' sensations. In a nutshell, in this affective communication, the most unaffected symptoms, such as Malvina's and Ludomir's bodily postures or facial expressions, the heroine's disturbed fluency of speech and her partner's eloquence, all collide with their self-censorship in terms of speech and etiquette.

In this conversation, for the first time, the tale moves constantly (within the plot segments which it covers) towards spaces where the actions and utterances of the protagonists are situationally objectified, thereby emphasising the double-track affective communication which is taking place in the circumstances. This is why, as it unfolds, the plot will continue to convey the affection revealed by Malvina and Ludomir under various pretexts. Their affection will be communicated most obviously either in utterances and actions purposefully chosen by the protagonists themselves as symbolic, allegorical or allusive; or, vice versa, in utterances and actions whose symbolism or clear expressive quality springs from obvious, though instantaneously concealed spontaneous sources. The coded "messages", which Ludomir and Malvina address to each other and decode by means of language acts, are in the former case predetermined, and carefully rehearsed down to every detail, but in the latter – conversely – they emerge as if on the spur of the moment, as if unpremeditated, at the moment of the utterance being made, under the pressure of emotions arising together with the messages used to communicate them. I label the language acts which accompany the formulation of the latter type of coded messages "quasi-momentary" and "quasi-unpremeditated". Unlike the former type, through these language acts, the protagonists express what they really feel at the time ("in this moment", 37) and unexpectedly ("keenly", 37). This does not however occur without conscious, deliberate symbolisation on their part, conveyed by intonational qualities of speech (see the quotation below, particularly the phrase "with inexpressible feeling", 38, as a definition of the way in which a message is formulated).

The first category of messages bearing hidden meanings, or – as we have said before – coded messages, includes two symbols created by Ludomir for the benefit of Malvina. One is the *tableau vivant* which depicts the indestructible pact between Friendship and Love. The other is the inscription on a stone which verbally clarifies the living allegory and relates its significance to Malvina's life. Both anticipate the emotional fulfilment which will be corroborated in Malvina's life. It must be stressed that the protagonists' readiness to be affected by symbols, just like the earlier creation of the symbols, is part of a larger phenomenon, namely the protagonists' inclusion of the language of nature, i.e. the language of the natural environment around them, into the realm of emotional expression. Particularly beautified and idealised, it becomes their "language" of words. Hence it is not with their own language, but with the language of the poetic idyll that the landscapes of the garden, the river or the meadow, speak to the participants in Malvina's name-day celebration, herself included. Both symbols, i.e. the live allegory and the inscription in stone, are constituents of this idyllic language. In view of this, attention must be paid to the allusive connotations of "Ludomir's meadow" (162).

The function of the other category of messages, whose meanings are coded and concealed, is fulfilled by the epithet "Ungrateful". For Malvina and Ludomir, it is a means of identification: it establishes a thread of the most profound personal sympathy between them in three very different situations. On the first occasion, it appears at the moment when the narratorial tale connects the tide of events to the "declaration of love", even before the epithet is ever used by the protagonists themselves:

> In this moment Malvina felt keenly in her heart just how much she loved Ludomir. Unable to comprehend how Ludomir could not have suspected it, she allowed the word to escape from her lips: "Ungrateful!" Then, as she heard the people getting closer, she only had time to flee as fast as her legs would carry her. In her haste she forgot her veil, sodden with tears.
>
> "Ungrateful!" repeated Ludomir with inexpressible feeling. Seizing Malvina's veil he pressed it to his heart and said with ardour:
>
> "May I never part with it except with my life". (37–38)

Literally speaking, the epithet "Ungrateful" is a complaint from Malvina on account of the alleged lack of emotional response from Ludomir, but it in fact reveals a truth glimpsed in its paradoxical refutation. This epithet does not work straightforwardly; when she utters the word, the heroine voices something different from what it really means; by turning the complaint around, it offers the hero a complete understanding of the situation in which they both find themselves. For these reasons, the epithet becomes for them a word charged with more meanings than any other word or words that might explain their situation in clearer terms, and thus becomes fixed in their memories for good.

The protagonists' reception of accurate, though coded or concealed, meanings is assisted by non-verbal factors, either spontaneously located in the utterances formulated by them, or added to these utterances from the outside. These factors include the manner of articulation and intonation, gestures, and any other factors that contribute – through the mediacy of the characters' senses – to the contextualisation of particular utterances within the "live" diversity of moments and places in which they occur. The tale, with its primary focus on the characters' utterances that manifest themselves situationally, aloud and audibly, emphasises and identifies these extra-verbal factors, which enable the protagonists to influence each other with meanings that they are not able or willing to express verbally. The tale emphasises these through portraying obvious affective disturbances or highlighting certain features in their speech. It also identifies them by providing additional explanation when the weight of sympathy, which they are meant to inspire, is shifted to bodily postures, facial expressions, gestures, accompanying physical objects, acts attending speech, or anything else that agitates the protagonists mentally in a particular moment and place. Here, I refer to the already discussed dialogue between Malvina and Ludomir, in which the sympathy between them springs from the twice repeated epithet "Ungrateful", and the scene in which Ludomir delivers his monologue (Malvina keeps silent throughout), although in reality she provides affective responses in this non-verbal dialogue which appears to be taking place between the two of them:

> Hearing her voice he ran to where she was sitting, unobserved by her. But when she stopped singing Ludomir, his heart too full for his reason to maintain the slightest control over it, completely lost his head and fell at Malvina's feet, unable to say anything but:
> "I have frightened you, Malvina! Ah! Spare me!... Forgive me... but I am so unhappy!"
> Malvina, alarmed, confused, was speechless. (36–37)

At this point, some historical and theoretical information must be given in order to elucidate these two conversations between Wirtemberska's protagonists. In the most influential eighteenth-century European works on language and human communication through language, which continued to affect the understanding of these phenomena in the early nineteenth century, non-verbal factors were singled out and widely debated as additional means of expression supporting verbal utterances. In his *L'Essai sur l'origine des langues,* Rousseau drew attention to their paradoxical nature and labelled them "mute eloquence" (1998, 291). He also pointed to the existence of numerous communicative situations, in which these non-verbal factors played a decisive role as sources of information about the content of verbal utterances. Among them, he distinguished those meant to "mov[e] the heart and enflam[e] the passions" (1998, 291). Rousseau's interest in non-verbal communication, as well as in the significance of non-verbal (mute) factors in verbal communication mediated through the voice, was by no means exceptional either in the eighteenth century or at the turn of the nineteenth. In discussions of these issues, the science of rhetoric was also useful, particularly in the field of the so-called *actio*, which standardised "the orator's use of voice, gesture and facial expression, as appropriate under the circumstances" (Okopień-Sławińska 1988, 433; trans. M.O.), or – to quote another formulation – "corporeal exteriorization of discourse" (Barthes 1998, 66). It should be noted that since Antiquity, the rules codified under the *actio* pertained equally to rhetorical speech, dramatic performance and recitation (see Aristotle's *Rhetoric*, Book III). This explains why the above-mentioned work by Ludwik Osiński presents this very view on non-verbal factors in speech, which is surprisingly concurrent with Rousseau's ideas, especially when it comes to accentuating their paradoxical nature. Osiński, after Rousseau, highlights this very feature:

> The sound of voice, the look in the eye, the expression of the character: do they not portray desire and passion as well as words do? Let us state this clearly: are these silent signs not frequently even more expressive than words? Sometimes one facial expression or eye movement, or one exclamation drawn from the overflowing heart, may have more impact than speech. This language cannot be replaced by the elaborate sound of words, because it is a natural language, an instinctive reflection of human needs and affections, understood equally by all. (1862, 195; trans. M.O.)

Let us note that Osiński differentiates between "the sound of voice" and "the elaborate sound of words" (1862, 195). He classifies the former with the "silent signs", possibly in view of its potential to contribute its own non-verbal meanings to the utterances which are formulated on its basis.

It may safely be said that the affective communication as presented by Wirtemberska reflects the merging, or, as we would say today, functional combination of speech, expressive intonation or pauses, and non-verbal communication. I wish to stress this because the study of language at the turn of the nineteenth century, represented by the above-mentioned works, demonstrates that the co-existence of these phenomena in non-rhetorical, colloquial speech was only beginning to attract scholarly attention. The arguments of Zofia Florczak concerning pre-romantic theories of language enable us to conclude that the expansion in scholarly attention to language was enhanced by growing interest in the "sonic aspect of language", alongside that of "how emotions are expressed in utterances" (Florczak 1978, 63; trans. M.O.). Here we may recall, after Yuri Lotman (1978, 227), Rousseau's fascination with intonation as a constituent of utterance, which combines the emotional (i.e. the natural) with the rational (i.e. the conventional). Lotman also points to Rousseau's parallel fascination with "child paralinguistics", and draws on this argument presented in a passage of Rousseau's *Émile*:

> All our languages are works of art. Whether there was a language natural and common to all men has long been a subject of research. Doubtless there is such a language, and it is the one children speak before knowing how to speak. [...] It is not the sense of the word that children understand but the accent which accompanies it. To the language of the voice is joined that of gesture, no less energetic. This gesture is not in children's weak hands; it is on their visages. [...] Accentuation is the soul of speech. It gives speech sentiment and truth. Accentuation lies less than the word does. (Rousseau 1979, 65–72)

Below is Herder's argument which likewise reflects a fascination with the emotional sound of an utterance and the simultaneous problem of conveying it through writing:

> When [the sounds] get articulated and get spelled out on paper as interjections, then the most opposed sensations have almost a single expression. The dull "Ah!" is both a sound of melting love and a sound of sinking despair; the fiery "Oh!" is both an eruption of sudden joy and an eruption of impetuous fury, both of rising admiration and of welling lamentation. But do these sounds exist in order to be depicted on paper as interjections, then? (2004, 67)

What else needs to be said about the tale's initial tension between Malvina and Ludomir's close proximity, which enables them to feel the spontaneity of their behaviours and responses, and the reliance of both of them on indirectness and ambiguity in demonstrating their reciprocity of feeling? First of all, that manifestations of the absolute psychological reciprocity between Malvina and Ludomir are tainted with indefiniteness, uncertainty and unfulfilment. The narrator's awareness of this begs the question which she articulates in the moment immediately before both their reciprocal but "indirect" declaration of love, and their explicit declaration. Here is the narrator's question:

> Now that the Reader has read what has transpired so far, I wonder what you have made of it. Was Ludomir in love with Malvina? Was Malvina in love with Ludomir? (29–30)

It must also be said that, when it comes to the essence of the affective relationship between Malvina and Ludomir, the impression of unclarity, uncertainty and indefiniteness is maintained due to yet another factor. The thing that constantly depends on the protagonists' alternating shifts between the concealment and camouflaging of their affections (i.e. ambivalent declarations) on the one hand, and, on the other, the genuine experience of these affections (i.e. understanding the hidden meanings of symbols, allegories and allusions; grasping the meanings of speech utterances on the basis of situational, and – according to today's criteria – associated non-verbal psychological factors), is the riddle *sensu stricto*. The riddle, on the one hand, is the mystery which shrouds Ludomir's origins; on the other, it is the fact that Malvina finds herself confronted by that very riddle. At times, the relationship between Malvina and Ludomir borders on a "psychological" riddle; at other times, on a "real-life" one. The ties which bind these two strands together are Ludomir's pleas not to have to reveal his life story and his brief hints, such as the already quoted "but I am so unhappy!" (37).

In this way, the progress of the tale covering the events before Ludomir's disappearance from Krzewin, i.e. the initation of the novel's plot through an accumulation of unknowns, forms the basis for the protagonists' reliance on what they themselves refer to as "imagining" (13). Considering the initial course of events, this cognitive process must be called the "heart's intuition" of one individual about the other individual's reciprocity. As the tale unfolds and the Warsaw events are narrated, following another meeting between Malvina and Ludomir, it appears that these "imaginative" and "intuitive" processes are only half the story. At this point, however, my analysis of the tale must be interrupted in order to define what the letters contribute to the tale, what event-related aspects expand the reality presented so far, and finally what meaningful qualities enhance the protagonists' language acts, since they constitute the most important factor of this very reality.

The Protagonists' Letters as Images of the Written Word Arising from their Withdrawal from the Sphere of the Spoken Word and Meanings Thereby Conveyed

The letters, i.e. the material word and accessories to the plot, belong with the settings of the aristocratic country house, the salon and the city, towards which the narrative shifts. They serve to inform readers about what happens in between these spaces and the inner lives ("hearts") of the protagonists, concealed from their eyesight and hearing. In the tale which follows the situation-based, non-secret and audible speech of the protagonists, the letters – functioning as accessories to the plot, and as an additional means of narrative conveyance of information, carve out enclaves of communicative withdrawal and secrecy, highlighting the protagonists' privacy and emotional secrets. Three times in the course of the whole plot, from out of the home and family space, as well as out of that of the city and salon, loom the figures of Ludomir and Malvina, entirely absorbed either in the writing of a letter to their one and only reader, or in the reading of a letter from their one and only letter writer. Both activities are visible to nobody but themselves. Ludomir and Malvina are then shown as individuals leading their inner lives, and jealously guarding the exclusivity of their psychological experiences related to the letters being read or written.

This is how Ludomir comes to understand the incoherence of acts attending the writing of a letter:

> I cannot write any more; perhaps in a while I will be calmer and manage to finish my letter, but now it is not in my power to even add one word more. (39)

Various forms of inner separation from her family surroundings are planned and undertaken by Malvina in order for her to be able to secretly experience the sensations related to her beloved. She omits to mention having had a letter from him, which results in its content being kept secret. She braces herself for anticipated remarks from those around her on the subject of her beloved's contemptible behaviour. Finally, she adopts an air of indifference meant to mislead her companions:

> She felt clearly that to converse frequently about Ludomir, to reveal her inner sorrow and to share it with others were the surest ways of nourishing feelings and thoughts that caution advised her to suppress. This thought affected her

mind so powerfully that she undertook immediately to make no mention of Ludomir's letter. Yet love and not caution was the truer motive for this undertaking, instilling in Malvina's heart a kind of jealousy and a desire that nobody except herself should know his feelings, suffer because of his sufferings, pine for him after he had departed, or know the reason for his departure.

Furthermore Malvina was afraid of hearing remarks repeated which might justifiably be made regarding Ludomir's mysterious behaviour and which for her would be intolerable, since they cast an unpleasant shadow over his conduct. And Malvina feared the dark shadow surrounding everything that affected Ludomir.

All these reasons taken together meant that Malvina did violence to her own feelings, something that was not easy for her to bear. Managing to hide her grief and the true condition of her heart, and assuming an air of indifference, she went downstairs to the dining-room where her aunt and sister were already waiting for her at the breakfast table. (44–45)

Then there is the additional situation in which a small scrap of a letter received from Ludomir, although not addressed to Malvina, places her in direct contact with a message written in his hand, at the same time inexplicably denying her access to the letter's content:

The coins that Ludomir had thrown in the day before also fell out; on the piece of paper in which they were wrapped Malvina recognised his handwriting. We might forgive her for staring at this scrap of paper with curiosity. It was a fragment of a letter written in his own hand but unfinished; in many places the words had been erased and a whole chunk of the letter had been torn out. After patiently studying the few confused lines for a long time, Malvina was able to decipher: "...unhappy as never before..." [...]. It is not hard to imagine Malvina's amazement when she read these words. She surmised that the draft letter had not been sent and had been used, no doubt inadvertently, as wrapping paper. But to whom had the letter been written? Who was this beloved mother, to whom Ludomir addressed expressions of tender feeling as well as an outpouring of all his woes with such total, as far as Malvina could ascertain, trust and confidence? What were these woes? The whole thing seems impossible to understand or comprehend. (104–105)

Taken jointly, the letters present in the tale as accessories to the plot and as narrative means for pushing it forward, are to be viewed primarily as manifestations of the protagonists' withdrawal from situation-based, non-secret and spoken-aloud communication, i.e. from familiar, or conversational and affective, or conversational and salon-based, speech. Conversely, it could be stated that they provide evidence of the speakers' shift towards individuated communication, mainly personal, but also confidential and secret, which occurs via the written word addressed to their closest or most trusted individuals.

At this juncture, it must also be said that contemporary aestheticians also remarked on the equivalent yet antithetical relationship between conversation and letters. In 1786, Franciszek Bohomolec pointed out that these two forms of communication could be viewed in identical terms although they were meant for different recipients, the present and the absent respectively: "For the letter is nothing but the same speech addressed to an absent person which might be delivered to them if present" (1967, 223; trans. M.O.). In his 1826 definitions of the letter, Euzebiusz Słowacki aimed to demonstrate the parallels and simultaneous distinctiveness of both these forms: "A letter, to be precise, is a conversation between persons who are separated by distance. It is written word in place of spoken word, necessary for reasons of friendship, confidence, politeness or other interpersonal relations" (1826, 21; trans. M.O.).

I accept that, as suggested by the novel itself – as well as by the above discussions, that the moments when the letters enter the tale, i.e. at certain points in the plot, as well as their content, are first and foremost determined by the letters' being the result of their authors' defiance of the situational objectification of the spoken word. The letters are a special form of dialogic exchange between the protagonists, which, due to the exclusion of the voice feature of speech, do not have to be complemented by censoring situational gestures. As a result, they can contain material – externalised, verbalised or even expressed reflectively, and thus made more profound – which was not able, or would not have been able, to become part of spoken utterance due to the said censorship.

For these reasons, to their authors, the letters function as sites for pondering past conversations, both those in which the characters participated through real speech and those in which they were merely listeners. In other words, the letters are sites for re-living the memories of psychological experiences or emotional states, which had previously provided the rationale for active co-participation in language acts, or conversely – for lack of such participation. The presence of the letters allows both the original acts and states, and memories of them, to be revealed in connection with particular events and situations.

It is only the letters therefore that enable us to observe how, importantly, the protagonists' spoken utterances are absorbed into their memory. After being internally experienced, such utterances are pondered in letters, together with a whole range of minor details which remain hidden from everyone but themselves. This is due to the spoken-aloud, hence audible, quality of the protagonists' speech. These are the properties which form the basis for the situational objectification of these utterances (alongside the feelings expressed via this medium).[15] This fact informs the protagonists' (Ludomir's and, more importantly, Malvina's) affective experiences, language acts and behaviours hidden from others. The letters written by the two main characters and, more precisely, the declarations contained in them validate the existence of this concealed sphere of emotions which is thereby created between the protagonists, at the same time expressing those very emotions.

I shall now endeavour to analyse a representative case of one unrevealed thought of Malvina's. The thought is expressed and discussed by the heroine in a letter to her sister, which is where it can be cited from. But in the main dialogue, reproduced in the letter, or to be precise, in the epistolary dialogue, it never sees the light of day. It emerges spontaneously, from Malvina's being enchanted by the sound of Ludomir's voice, and then comes to be expressed in affectively dramatised words. A moment before being voiced, the thought is censored, questioned and internalised by the heroine. As a result, it never reaches Ludomir, although it was originally intended for him and addressed to him. With this thought, Malvina dismisses, against the prevailing opinion of others, any possible change in Ludomir's feelings for her and in hers for him. If spoken out loud by Malvina, it would have made an absolutely open declaration of the kind Malvina had never made to Ludomir. He had made one to her, although not aloud – but in a letter. Thus restrained and internalised, to Malvina, the thought becomes the first symptom of the loss of their complete sympathy, which to her had justified the declaration she had intended to make. From this point of view, quoting this very thought in a letter to her sister, and retelling – at a temporal distance – the event which had made the thought emerge, while she prevents it from seeing the light of day, must be viewed as another symptom of Malvina's sense of loss of complete sympathy. It is this sympathy which she had meant to convey in reality and whose confirmation she had hoped to see in the other person. I have taken as the motto to this chapter of my study

---

15 Cf. this fragment from Malvina's letter: "Wanda, I am abusing your patience describing the tiniest details of yesterday evening. But alas! Tiny details sometimes mean the difference between happiness and unhappiness. A friendly glance, a cold stare – sometimes contain within themselves absolute heaven or absolute despair" (58–59).

the very thought in question quoted in the letter, confirming the fact that the thought is never revealed by Malvina in any other way. Here, I see it as a constituent part of the novel's plot, which complicates (working against the heroine) all the previous events, at the same time determining their further course, advantageous to her. After all, the thought arises in Malvina at the very moment when affective stimulation disrupts her cognitive capacity, to the extent that she makes a desired but essentially mistaken (something she does not know at the time) identification of two separate (in fact twin) persons, Prince Melsztyński and Ludomir. The thought is suppressed by the heroine in the very next moment, as she awakens to a sense of difference in two separate motivational subtexts ruling the thoughts and speech of Ludomir in the past – and now, in the present. As this thought takes shape, so does her cognitive failure concerning the person of Prince Melsztyński. Yet when the thought is suppressed, the cognitive truth concerning the inclination of Malvina's own heart is rediscovered despite her mistake. The further course of events abounds with the interweaving of these two processes: Malvina's continuing to be mistaken and her attempts to learn the truth. Moreover, in this thought, and in particular in the transition she makes from a conversational salon dialogue to the epistolary and the personal, I see a major justification for the conclusions I shall draw. Hence, in order to be able to discuss it at length, let me quote the passage in a context broader than before:

"Allow me to present to Lady S***," the Sheriff said to me, "young Prince Melsztyński, who desires most earnestly to make her acquaintance."

"Provided fate and circumstance don't conspire against it," the Prince interrupted, "I am sure I will not be the last of those competing to worship the new deity, of which Warsaw has recently taken possession."

Wanda! Ludomir's voice, which has so much power over my being, those precious tones, which I have not heard for so many months, then took control of my senses, and at that moment I forgot all Ludomir's faults and almost said with the sincerity of my former attachment: "Ludomir, surely people are blackening your name saying you no longer love Malvina – Malvina, who will never be able to forget you!"

But, Wanda, Prince Melsztyński's elegant compliment was so unlike Ludomir's delicate silence at Krzewin, so unlike his expressions which breathed the most ardent love. That compliment, I tell you, made me tremble, and the words I was about to utter froze on my lips. (57–58)

None of the Krzewin scenes of the meetings and conversations between Malvina and Ludomir, presented by the narrator, and none of my interpretations of these scenes, demonstrates better where the genuine expression of their reciprocal affections was (literally) hidden and what spheres of personal and spoken expression it included. Malvina's dual reaction, i.e. her inner response to Prince Melsztyński's voice and simultaneous rejection of his words, draws a clear dividing line between two aesthetic systems. One of them renders Malvina sensitive to the mere sound of the well-known voice, despite the fact that it carries no verbal content or form. The other is its exact opposite: it makes her completely insensitive to the conventional (in words and content) comparison of herself to "the new deity, of which Warsaw has recently taken possession" (57). The fact that Prince Melsztyński's voice exerts irresistible control over Malvina has its origin in individually and personally construed manifestations of the love which Ludomir had cherished for her. The representation of this affection accompanies the stifling of the declaration formulated by her. Its overpowering strength flows towards Malvina out of silence and voice-nuanced speech, or more precisely – from the wealth of its natural affective constituents. It could be said that Malvina negates the aesthetics of the compliment in as much as she herself is in love, animated by the aesthetics of the words and the voice, if we can put it that way. This means that Ludomir's words, spoken aloud and modulated, were to her more complete sources of information about his affection than their purely verbal matter. It also means that the presence of non-verbal elements in Ludomir's declarations and their impact on the truthfulness of his words reinforces Malvina's acceptance of his overall psychological and emotional stance. The compliment which she receives from Prince Melsztyński becomes to her a sign of the loss of that affection, and consequently – of that stance as well.

In the above-quoted fragment from Malvina's letter, we are dealing – significantly – with a case of the retelling of an event related to an unmade declaration, and not with a case of the restraint and internalisation of the affective language act itself. This may be because, in this supplementary epistolary account of the event by the heroine, the primary and secondary affective elements (the heroine's direct experiences of the sound of a voice and, conversely, the obsessive sensations brought on by the memory of this sound) and the intellectual elements (the heroine's mental and written references to the sensations provoked by the sound of the voice) are inseparable. Delineated by the epistolary account of the declaration's secrecy, the heroine's inner boundary between the "heart" and "reason" becomes more visible. It separates what stems from the heroine's sensual response to the quality of a voice from what stems from her use of the written word: intentional, consciously intuited with a view to controlling those instinctive qualities. Unlike the heart in the heroine's experience, the reason – manifested in the letters, fulfils the function of verbal opposition to the voice, i.e. writing. To the heroine, it offers understanding of her emotion rather than the manifestations of it that she experiences. To her, the latter are connected with the nuanced, tonal meanings of Ludomir's speech. It could even be said that whatever is natural, sensual and instinctive in Malvina's inner experience, whatever runs against the external convention of concealment and masking of feelings which she herself consciously implements, is associated by Malvina with the unique, individuated voice of Ludomir – to be precise, with the sound quality of that voice in its pure form unburdened by meaning, which allows her to re-affirm her opinion of Ludomir himself. It should be stressed that when, in her epistolary account, Malvina presents her emotional confusion as a result of the contradictory impressions which affect her: ranging from the most heated ("Melsztyński's elegant compliment was so unlike Ludomir's delicate silence [...] [or] the most ardent love", 57) to the coolest ("That compliment [...] made me tremble, and the words I was about to utter froze on my lips", 58), she in fact juxtaposes the "heated" quality accompanying the tonal, almost breathing, articulation of an emotion, experienced in the past, with the "iciness" of her current state of mind, due to the absence of the former qualities. In terms of her inner experience, this dramatic reversal in the quality of affective stimulation from "heated" to "icy" represents the preponderance of reason, as a cognitive alternative, over the heart. In other words, the act of letter writing replaces the spoken-aloud utterance as an alternative cognitive "tool" in the heroine's inner experiences, with regard to the feelings that dominate them.

The plot complications created in *Malvina* surrounding the discrepancy felt by the heroine between the sound quality of the hero's voice and his style of speech are so unusual and intriguing, they beg more general reflection. Let me now return to the issue of the vocal and intonational shaping of an utterance, coded within the rhetorical realm of the *actio*, as discussed by Rousseau and Herder.

The *actio* was a safeguard of consistency between the vocal and intonational aspect of an utterance and the feelings expressed by that utterance, such as outrage or sympathy. For formal public utterances, three aspects of speech mattered most: the volume of sound, the modulation of pitch, and rhythm (Aristotle n.d., 137). Rousseau and Herder, in turn, viewed *actio* in connection with the diversity and complexity of popular communicative behaviours, whose constituent it became. This preoccupation, i.e. with the close connection between speech and human intellectual or emotional stances, was precisely what Wirtemberska's novel used as the source of its plot complications. For Rousseau, the issue of vocal and intonational diversification and nuancing of utterances constituted the basis of human relationships. On the one hand, for him, it was the source of the utterance's content-based significance; on the other, it was a guarantee of its internal intellectual consistency. Rousseau, as already quoted, stated: "Accentuation is the soul of speech. It gives speech sentiment and truth. Accentuation lies less than the word does" (1979, 72). To justify this view, he added: "From the practice of saying everything in the same tone came the practice of mocking people without their being aware of it. The proscribed accentuation is succeeded by ways of pronunciation which are ridiculous, affected, and subject to fashion, such as one notices particularly in the young people of the court" (Rousseau 1979, 72). And then, in order to describe a person of exaggerated speech and behaviour, he said: "Instead of accentuating his speech, his affected language insinuates his meaning" (Rousseau 1979, 72). Let us note that a similar kind of speech failure triggers the plot complications in Wirtemberska's novel. The hero's utterance, rather than genuine feeling, comes across to the heroine as a salon caricature of itself. As a result, rather than receive this utterance holistically, as a set of impressions affecting her, Malvina experiences its breakdown into two contrasting parts: the vocal (sounds) and the verbal (meanings).

Having analysed a fragment of one letter, let me now move on to general remarks about the letters taken jointly. I wish to stress that, regardless of what their authors write about – whether it is events in which they participated, their experiences and emotions ("the conditions of her heart", 35), or matters subject to familial or salon secrecy, they do so in ways that could not be used in in family or social milieus that is in verifiable situations. If they relate events in which they participated, they emphasize their own role in these events and their own view of them (as in Ludomir's and Malvina's letters). If they confess their emotions or declare them to another, they do this so openly that, despite the fact that these confessions and declarations are made in writing, they seem to convey the immediacy of their emotional stirrings and desires. This is done totally independently of the censoring influence of contemporary speech conventions or etiquette (as in Ludomir's letters to his mother and to Malvina). If they convey confidential information, requests or commands, the characters take advantage of the lack of spoken communication with the addressee in order to create tension between the almost instinctive provision of information on past or present events and the message which they wish to communicate to the addressee. They act as if they were keen on spoken communication with the addressee in order to interest and provoke them to participate in the events (as in Wanda's and Lissowski's letters).

Above all, however, the letters of the protagonists, Ludomir and especially Malvina, testify equally to their communicative intentions with regard to their addressees and to their own self-reflective attitudes. This happens because the letters are, as I have already suggested, sites for the protagonists to ponder their roles in familial and salon-based communications, from the dictates of which they are only able to liberate themselves thanks to letters. This is also because their pondering becomes for the protagonists, a "tool" for thinking about their changing life circumstances, as was the case with Malvina's letter about her suppressed confession. The fact that Malvina, the author of a sequence of letters, acquires a deepened awareness of the mysterious inconstancy of Prince Melsztyński-Ludomir's mental and emotional attitude in comparison to the one demonstrated in the past, is closely connected to the type of epistolary communication that she carries on. This includes both its secretive nature, notwithstanding the intended purpose of that communication, and its individuation aimed at communication beyond the formality and conventionality of the salon. Yet it must be remembered that these complementary characteristics are also manifestations or symptoms of the written nature of epistolary communication in general.

Let us note that the written quality that renders an epistolary utterance confidential or even secretive does not remove its distinctive features as a spoken utterance, i.e. its addressing a recipient and referencing the outside world. At the same time, it enables materialisation of mental processes representative of the sender's self-reflective stance. Hence the written quality is the distinctive feature of an epistolary utterance, and as such provides Malvina with an opportunity to ponder and remember her experiences connected with events in which she participated, given her complete withdrawal from the spoken word through which they had occurred. At the same time, the written quality of an epistolary utterance gives Malvina an opportunity to make present her current experience, called now into being within her under pressure of her past, relived, experience. Yet she no longer looks back to the past, but towards the future, confronting the overall obscurity of the situations which she recounts in her letters and which she is still reliving.

Let me justify this on the basis of the final section of the letter, which contains the suppressed declaration of love. I will also draw on a particular sequence of events that centres on the heroine's transition from a spoken exchange to the writing of the quoted letter.

Here is the first example. In the concluding section of Malvina's letter about her suppressed declaration, her reflection on the past event – which is being relived by her through this remembrance, as if at the actual moment when the event was occurring – turns into a confessional declaration, in which she reveals her disorientation and inability to determine her future emotional and mental stance:

> Wanda, I am abusing your patience describing the tiniest details of yesterday evening. [...] My Wanda! Now I know who he is, this strange, this mysterious Ludomir... or rather I don't know, I don't understand, I cannot comprehend anything that touches upon his fate or his conduct! But I remember that I owe him my life, that I solemnly promised him never to take any step towards discovering the secret that surrounds him. "You would only increase my misfortune most painfully": those were the words of his letter which I have before my eyes. Ah, Ludomir! stop loving me, love another even, do whatever you will! Malvina is capable of weeping in silence, of suffering alone and rejected, but never will she remind you, neither in her words nor in her deeds, that she even knew you once. [...] Forgive me, Sister, if I, confident of your indulgent friendship, have shared with you the burden and sorrow of my soul! It has not been in my power to hide my least feeling. But from now I will try... to what?... ah, I do not know myself! I do not know why I am alive, what I want, what I should do, what I am supposed to believe! There is turmoil in my thoughts, turmoil in my heart (58–59).

Let us note that the heroine uses her memory to connect to the past, and her expectation – to reach out to the future. Let us also note that the highest exclamatory force is to be found in the sentence which receives its impetus from the words of Ludomir's letter, directly addressed to him and not to the actual addressee of the letter. It is only the epistolary secrecy that makes possible the utterance of this exclamation – just like the dialogic exchange of Malvina's and Ludomir's words because only in the letter can this exclamation preserve the features of one-sidedness without losing its meaning as a reply within the lovers' dialogue. The exclamatory phrase is, after all, written down in a letter and not spoken aloud in a home or salon environment.

Now for the second example. The sequence of events which I intend to highlight in order to support my claim that letters give the protagonists opportunities to distance themselves from events and experiences formed through the spoken word, makes visible the formation of a link between the heroine's reflective stance and the epistolary acts which she undertakes. This claim should not be weakened by the fact that Malvina, when turning to letter writing, recreates in this way not only speech itself but also its style, and – more precisely – the speaker's psychological and moral stance: *Sermo tanquam persona ipse loquens*. Let us also note that this letter contains, apart from reflection on Malvina's memories, speculations related to the future:

> "Beautiful Malvina!" he said to her. "I know you are one of the circle of devout collectors. I expect you will not refuse me the happiness of sharing with you this pious pilgrimage and will permit me to present myself on your doorstep at ten tomorrow morning with this end in view."
>
> "You may spare yourself the trouble, Prince," replied Malvina with an extremely cold bow. "Our sense of duty and our way of perceiving things are so different for us ever to be able to share them."
>
> Having spoken these words, Malvina left. When she returned home and before going to bed, her head and heart brimming with the contradictory feelings inspired by the various events of the evening, she wrote a long letter to Wanda describing the entire evening and concluding with the following words:
>
> "Oh, my Wanda! Once again I repeat and am more convinced than ever that the fashionable world, with its bad examples, its bad company, can corrupt the best hearts, the most noble spirits very quickly! Who could have told me that the Ludomir, in whom I saw nothing but what honesty and delicacy could create, who held the fulfilling of his duties as the most agreeable obligation, who was always concerned with the happiness and pleasure of others, that this same Ludomir could, within such a short space of time, exchange these noble pursuits for a cold and sneering vanity that starves all good and tender emotions and for a nonchalance that everywhere seems to be a feature of fashionable society. Neither from conviction nor because of their attraction will Malvina ever find it in her to accept them". (73–74)

It would seem that the following conclusion can now be drawn: Malvina's letters are her constant companions in her confrontation with the mysterious inconstancy of her beloved. But, in effect, as the letters themselves become constituent parts of subsequent situations which they depict, the distinctiveness of their particular features varies. Let me discuss three selected manifestations of this.

In Malvina's letter about her unexpected meeting with Ludomir in Warsaw, the most important is the individuated, personal nature of the relationship which it depicts. This communicative quality stands in contradistinction to both social ceremomy and social intimacy, features of the milieu depicted in the letter. At the same time, this is the same communicative quality, in the name of which Malvina denies internally the possibility of a genuine heart-to-heart exchange with Ludomir Prince Melsztyński, and which itself creates a further emotional problem springing from a conversation that never occurred.

At first glance, in the above-quoted letter, of most significance seems to be its individuated, personal quality. Yet the reflection which it contains becomes a manifestation of the heroine's clearly articulated attitude towards the world of "a cold and sneering vanity [...] and [...] a nonchalance" (73–74), embodied by Prince Melsztyński. We need to recognise that this view is formulated by Malvina in writing, after she has fenced off the unwanted world, and – if we can put it like this – after her demonstrative withdrawal from the conversation she was part of in the world of which she does not approve.

To conclude, let me quote from one of Malvina's letters which I have not yet discussed. It recounts her encounter with the doubled, real and apparitional, figures of Prince Melsztyński-Ludomir. The most conspicuous properties of this letter are its mysterious content and confidential nature.[16] The domination of these qualities corresponds to the "supernatural", as Wirtemberska put it, course of the conversation that is being recounted. In the events presented in this letter, all the plot's earlier indications of Malvina's lover's inconstancy reach culmination. These events disturb her mentally ("I suddenly saw Ludomir's image reproduced behind him", says the heroine in this letter, 137).

In this way, as a result of the distinct stylistic variations found in Malvina's subsequent letters, the mismatch between the indications of

---

16 Cf. the postscript to this letter by Malvina: "To you alone have I revealed the reason for my extreme terror at Wilanów as well as the effects of this fearful shock on my mind; everyone believes that that appalling scream was the only thing that frightened me; I therefore implore and beseech you never to mention it, for otherwise I may be painfully forced to recognise that what for me was all too real has been taken by others to be but the hallucination of a far too vivid imagination, or some kind of false dissembling" (138).

love, as demonstrated to her by Prince Melsztyński-Ludomir, and his mental and moral attitude, as she remembered it and which, used to validate his affection, are shown as a cognitive process invisible to the salon company, one that occurs within the heroine yet demands that she continue to participate in situations arranged by that company. The object of cognition here is the emotion locked in the heroine's heart. Let us note that the more forceful her opposition to the salon company and its social life, to the mental and moral stance of Ludomir Prince Melsztyński, typified by his disregard for the ideas which she herself embraces as well as his emotional inconstancy (Doryda, Florynka), the more actively she tries to discover what makes him persist in his affection for her. This is made possible by the skills which Malvina acquires when shifting from conversations to acts of letter writing. Conversations, manifestations of speech, and letters, manifestations of writing, are both specific cognitive paths which promote feeling and thinking.

Let us note that the position in which the heroine finds herself makes her, as I have tried to demonstrate, accept one person's heart's intuition about another's heart's reciprocity as the basis of a one-sided problem, namely one person's striving to intuit the causes of her own heart's stirrings. It seems that the cognitive process which the heroine followed within, as I have argued above, pertains to her very shift from one to the other category of intuition. It also seems that the two meanings of the word "intuition", which the writer most likely had in mind when creating the eponymous metaphor of "the heart's intuition", need to be taken into account here. It is interesting that the association of the heart as a symbol of feeling with intuition as a symbol of a mental act was a concept to which Jan Śniadecki actually objected:

The author wished to refer to the heart's struggle with appearance and sense by subtitling the book "The Heart's Intuition". But "intuition" is not a Polish word, and the Polish equivalent, "domysł" ["imagining"] pertains to an act of reasoning, not feeling. The heart sighs, warms to another, burns, feels, but it does not intuit. Better would be, it seems to me, to call this the inspiration, accuracy, complexity, or foreknowledge of the heart. Having shown so much beauty and power of language, the author ought not to offend it with a foreign word, one that defies accuracy and precision of thought. (Śniadecki 2003, 28; trans. M.O.)

Part Two
Heart and Thoughts

There are steps there at the edge of the waves,
Where for the first time we admitted with our lips
That we had long loved with our hearts.
– Juliusz Słowacki, *"In Switzerland"*

Repetition and Continuity

The time has come to view the tale and the letters, *Malvina*'s two contrasting and interweaving narrative forms, jointly rather than – as before – in
isolation. It is time to take a more careful look at the dual presentation of
events and at the events themselves. It is time to take up those hitherto
undeveloped threads in my analysis that highlight the roles of the tale
and the letters other than those I have already outlined.

I have so far viewed the tale as a form of communication designed to
present the story of the protagonists' amorous relationship and focused
on their behaviours, punctuated with spoken-aloud, situation-based,
conspicuous utterances. At the same time, the tale is a communication
which shares with the heroine's letters (i.e. with her unspoken, non-situ-
ational, inconspicuous communications) the function of informing the
reader about the emotional dilemma which she has gone through, i.e.
about only a part of that tale. But its telling is not limited to the representational and communicative acts which it performs. The starting point
to the interpretative acts performed by it are the narrator's reflections on
affection and happiness. The generally accepted opinions on these topics
clash with the wisdom that the narrator has acquired from the vicissitudes
of life as experienced by her characters. Her reflections on affection and
happiness as an interpretative code, as we would put it today, accentuate

the ethical dimension of the dilemma which needs to be solved by the heroine, and at the same time of the baffling events in which the dilemma has its source.

I have analysed the letters, particularly those written by the heroine, as messages which complement the tale with content located cryptically within the course of events. I have highlighted the fact that although the letters function within the tale as messages that make the content visible, they also work within the plot as consequences of hidden epistolary acts. I have linked their occurrence to the protagonists' withdrawal from spoken-aloud, conspicuous communications, in which their utterances are censored and brought to the attention of third persons. And hence to their withdrawal from the communicative space dominated by spoken-aloud situation-based utterances, thus removing any features of spontaneity. I have offered a detailed analysis of one of Malvina's letters, in which she recounts the moment of suppressing her own affective thought when confronted by her interlocutor's utterance under particular circumstances. In consequence, the thought is subject to virtual "remoulding" and ultimately loses all its vividness and directness. The letters have so far been, to me, a symptom of the protagonists' deliberate construction of individuated communicative acts which may counterbalance those that are spoken-aloud, situation-based and conspicuous. I have demonstrated that, just as Malvina forgoes expressing her thought but does not forgo thinking it, in the same way she forgoes certain spoken-aloud utterances in favour of epistolary ones, but she does not forgo her reliving of the spoken-aloud utterances in the epistolary ones. I have drawn attention to the fact that, in the letters, the protagonists' emotions and thoughts, although turned into monologues and thus muted, are nevertheless revealed. Yet in analysing the letters as utterances that function cryptically, I have not yet considered those moments in the plot when letters appear directly, as objects owned by one of the protagonists, arousing other characters' interest due to the otherwise unrevealed content they contain. This is precisely the kind of thing that brings us closer to solving the riddle which informs the course of events. Let me now give this issue my undivided attention.

In this part of my study, I hope to outline more precisely than before the role of the spoken and written narrative duality of *Malvina* in visualising the rift on the level of events between the external, i.e. subject to spoken-aloud utterances, and the internal, subject to those silent and cryptic utterances. I also hope to decode the symbolic intentions contained in the spoken and written aspects of the narrative and in the narrator's reflections on affection and happiness. It seems that these symbolic intentions, since they correspond to the same type of intentions signalled in the chapter titles and in the title of the entire novel, introduce a sense of balance or even stability to the presented reality of inconstant affections, beliefs and utterances: this is what constitutes their ethical quality.

The Warsaw Plot

My analysis will enable an insight into the hitherto undiscussed Warsaw section of the *Malvina* plot. As in the rest of the plot, its event-related tension springs from the dual narrative mode of the novel. It is clear that neither the main nor the minor characters, in their mutual inter-actions, speak to or affect one another straightforwardly. After all, the interweaving of the tale and the letters invariably brings into focus the conflict between the two planes of the characters' lives: the visible (hence accessible to the eyesight and hearing of those around them) and the concealed (accessible only to the correspondents' eyes).

The complications of the Warsaw plot are also triggered by issues which loom large between the protagonists but are never articulated aloud. One of these is veiled by the protagonists' *written conversation*, while another takes the form of a *reading aloud* of a letter concerning the protagonists. Significantly, the former touches on the crux of the mystery central to the entire plot, while the latter serves to facilitate the resolu-tion of the mystery. It is also significant that the ultimate denouement is achieved through *a loosening of the characters' tongues*, which allows them to gain an understanding of Ludomir's childhood and parentage. As current events serve to elucidate the preceding ones, the running plot includes accounts of times past, such as letters which change hands, or family yarns. Let us note that the interweaving of the tale and the letters is what propels the plot according to a "rhythm" in which the protagonists shift from speaking aloud to muted speech, and vice versa. The purpose is either to conceal the intended meaning of utterances from others, or conversely – to reveal some hitherto concealed events or mysteries.

Here I point to one of *Malvina*'s most conspicuous distinctive fea-tures, derived from its narrative division into spoken and written word. From this observation follow important implications for this study – and for any study of *Malvina*, for that matter. One is that any analysis of this novel should include the narrated courses of events; another, less obvious, is that it ought to investigate what lies at very core of these courses.

In terms of structure, the Warsaw plot section is a masterpiece. It opens with the first Warsaw encounter between Malvina and Ludomir. This is when she simultaneously recognises and fails to recognise him as her beloved, and decides to suppress a confession meant for his ears. This part of the plot has it climax in the hitherto undiscussed encounter between Malvina and the two persons of her one beloved, when she breaks off in the middle of a sentence containing a promise. Here, the entire plot focuses on events which are as ambiguous as they are inexplicable.

To begin with, these transformations are manifested in Malvina's beloved's mental attributes and actions, which confuse the heroine (for instance, there is the sequence of events centred around the charity collection: at first, Ludomir embodies frivolity; next, sensibility; and then – recklessness or "neglect", 94). Furthermore, the subsequent events bring to Malvina's attention the inexplicable dualities in her beloved's physical being. For example, during the chivalric tournament, Ludomir is represented by two figures, communicated to Malvina by the mottos on their shields. Both mottos bear affective meaning which she recognises easily – hence both function as emblems of Ludomir. The plot complications reach a climax when, during a dark but moonlit night, Malvina confronts Ludomir's duality: two physically identical yet different persons (this brings to mind Apollo confronting the Androgynes, the four-armed and four-legged offspring of the Moon, split in half by Zeus, as Plato recounts in his *Symposium* [2008, 23–24]). At the same time, the encounter causes Malvina to stop short of finishing her promise of love, likewise splitting it into two parts, the uttered and the unuttered:

All these things taken together overwhelmed her soul and compelled her – I am able to say – to raise her eyes, give the Prince her hand and declare:

"Return safely, Prince, and when the war is over..."

But her words were cut short by an horrendous shriek as the most extraordinary apparition confounded her senses. In the dense thicket of the hedge, clearly illuminated by the moonlight, Malvina saw standing opposite her a second image of Ludomir. (131–132)

"Return safely, Prince, and when the war is over..." – were the words with which I answered Ludomir and to which I meant to add, "...and when the war is over, you will receive my hand." But I was unable to conclude these final words. My words were interrupted, interrupted perhaps forever, by an appalling scream and by a supernatural apparition, whose appearance dumbfounded my senses at the time, and whose memory has thrown me into a terrified panic ever since. I suddenly saw Ludomir's image reproduced behind him; despair and death were written on his face; he was lit up by the moonlight and seemed to emerge out of the darkness of the night. (136–137)

The Warsaw plot develops along these lines: the clearer the manifestations of Ludomir's changeability are felt by Malvina as a personal duality, the more keenly she perceives this inexplicable phenomenon as the loss of what she remembers as Ludomir's stable moral and mental constancy, fully embodied in his affections and fully informing his behaviour and speech even at the time when he shrouded both in secrecy. Such is the structural principle of the Warsaw plot. Sensing the difference in personality-related subtexts which propel Ludomir's changing spiritual stance, and pondering this very difference, becomes for Malvina a cognitive sign in its own right. It makes her uphold the imperative of psychological and moral constancy, alongside perfection, as foundations for emotional reciprocity. At the same time, it makes her ignore the affection which runs counter to this very imperative. This results from Malvina's differentiation between the essence of revealing the affections and the essence of the affections themselves. It is precisely against this background that the discrepancy, which she cannot not perceive, between the previous and current forms of Ludomir's affections makes her interpret them as mere salon insincerity.

I now wish to take a closer look at the structure of the Warsaw plot, and then explore the complications in the drama of the heroine's desired identification of the two different individuals, and her growing disappointment when their identity is gradually disproved. I am bound to do this, having expressed my belief that the spoken and written turns of *Malvina's* narration are interwoven with the events of the entire, and in particular – the Warsaw, plot. Likewise, I shall pursue my declared intention to discuss the symbolic purposes included in the twists and turns of the plot, as well as in the events themselves.

Unshaken or Unwavering Constancy?

The most important factor that makes Malvina experience the "division" into two of Ludomir is the changing affective and communicative ambience in which their meetings take place. This is what makes her respond either in a restrained manner: when she feels his absence despite his constant presence, or in an impulsive manner: when she feels his presence despite their scanty interaction.

The Warsaw salon eliminates from Malvina's and Prince Melsztyński-ki-Ludomir's behaviour the lively responsiveness which at Krzewin made their relationship genuinely spontaneous. In consequence, lost are the charm and appeal (Malvina calls them "attraction", 52) which used to resonate in their previous conversations through symbols, allusions or irony gently turned against the beloved (such as the label "Ungrateful"), as well as in the modulated voice and intonation of their exchanges. The Warsaw salon invites echoes of those former affective and communicative qualities, now largely weakened due to convention and derailed through trivial, familiar acts of propriety and politeness. The salon speech of the protagonists is tainted by Ludomir's public displays of affection for his intended, at the same time slighting her with his inconsiderate behaviour and moral precepts, and by Malvina's emotional restraint as a response to this affective "licentiousness".

Malvina's letters, in which she begins to understand what binds her to Ludomir (affection and her promise not to insist on solving the mystery) and what separates her from him (i.e. his psychological transformation) provide insights into the obscure aspects of her responses. During their meetings and conversations, she tends to suppress these aspects rather than allowing for their constant operation in all their suggestiveness and truth, thereby experiencing repeated failure.

In contrast, the meeting of the protagonists during the charity collection restores between them what Malvina has already considered lost: their sympathy expressed at once by means of situational details, half-broken exclamations, meaningful glances, and – more than anything else – the voice: "His gaze burned with the tenderest love, and in his voice Malvina could distinguish surprise, joy, emotion, as well as a slight hint of reproach" (88). Changed beyond recognition, Ludomir counters Malvina's impression that he is a member of the salon community, like Lissowski or Doryda, and that he plays the familiar role of a man of the world and a ladies' man. He dumbfounds Malvina with his transformation and puzzles her as an individual compelled to undergo regular personal transformations, thus strengthening her sense of an unfathomable mystery.

An external picture of Malvina's behaviour and responses at the salon is provided by the letters of Major Lissowski, one of Malvina's admirers. The letters express his admiration for her skilful ways of preserving her independence in a milieu which forces its participants to meet not only the requirements of propriety and familiarity, but also to engage in backbiting, the components of socially accepted standards of behaviour:

> I [...] am sometimes so impressed by Malvina's cold civility that I never allow myself in her company to use any of those expressions which severity would call "bad tone" but which we would call priceless elegance, or to indulge in any backbiting or unrestrained ranting or, in other words, to carry on any part of our normal mode of existence. (60)

The Warsaw plot develops in a way so ambiguous that Malvina's growing sense of Ludomir's "split self" is accompanied by what she rationally perceives as evidence of his personal identity. The moment of collision between the dilemma she faces and the manifestations of Ludomir's two different personalities is depicted in the scene in which they both communicate by means of coded speech and writing, exchanged while dancing and playing word-games in the salon. Let me now analyse the major structural and content-related components of the scene.

Thanks to a mirror, the eyes of Malvina and Ludomir meet unexpectedly. This breeds a feeling of intimacy between them, which was not there before. The glances and stirrings normally adjusted to the requirements of the circumstances are transformed into spontaneous responses. Malvina's question and Ludomir's answer, conveyed through their eyes as much as through their voices, contain coded messages. This is suggested by the narrator's explanation:

> Resting her chin in her hand, she stared into the mirror without thinking what she was doing; but then she caught sight not only of her own face but that of Ludomir, which she had not noticed before. His eyes were fixed upon her with almost that same expression of sensitivity and sadness, which had so captivated her at Krzewin and which she had sought in vain on the fickle countenance of Prince Melsztyński in Warsaw. She shuddered involuntarily and for the first time since her arrival in the city she addressed him first:
>
> "How come, Prince, you are not dancing this evening? You, who are usually in such high spirits, seem pensive?"
>
> "I wanted to dance, I would gladly have given half my life to dance, but nobody wanted me and nothing brings me luck."
>
> "Nobody" stood for Malvina; "nothing brings me luck" meant that she could not dance with him: thus the customary language of lovers, who encapsulate the whole world in the object of their love. (69–70)

Malvina and Ludomir, the main actors in this salon scene, not fully quoted or discussed here yet, present themselves to each other in the act of being moved by the situation they experienced before at Krzewin. The name of "Krzewin", a symbol of this experience, although not spoken aloud, appears to secretly stimulate their turning towards each other.

For the ways in which mirroring complicates the novel's entire plot, sometimes making Malvina's eyes see Prince Melsztyński as not-Ludomir, and at other times – as Ludomir, i.e. not-Prince-Melsztyński, this scene is crucial. It parallels, on the one hand, the previous scene of the protagonists' Warsaw meeting, when "in the person of" Prince Melsztyński Malvina observes and experiences Ludomir's simultaneous "similarity" and "otherness". It also anticipates the scene of their final Warsaw meeting, in which Malvina experiences most realistically the presence of the two doppelgänger incarnations of her beloved. The scene's central importance rests on the fact that it is the only scene featuring the leitmotif of Ludomir's embodiment in two strikingly different figures, and yet one and the same person.

The mysterious bond between their Krzewin and Warsaw experiences, engendered by the protagonists' more than usually intimate turn towards each other, manifests itself in the content of the question-and-answer quiz which they address to each other in writing during a salon game of *secrétaire*. The narrator, when discussing the game, summarises its secret benefits to the participants as "a splendid way of finding out what they did not wish to ask one another directly, or of explaining things they did not dare to utter" (70). During the second game, Malvina, using her right to the communicative initiative (and the secret nature of that very initiative) startles Ludomir with the question: "Did not last summer, did not last August / leave any lasting impression?" (71) According to the rules of *secrétaire*, Malvina's question ought to have played the role of the opening, interrogative, part of a certain type of a riddle, one that resembles a maxim in that it touches upon general issues, notions or moral values. When completed by the addressee, the next explanatory part of the riddle ought to expose his or her understanding of the internal issues raised in the original question. This is precisely the case with the enigmatic questions and answers formulated by other participants in the game, which the narrator quotes. Taken jointly, the questions and answers form internally dialogic sentences, maxims or, as we would say today, aphorisms:

How are charm and hatred alike?
Both are contained in a single glance.

With what does love light up her torch and then extinguish it?
With a sigh and tears.

What is the advantage and disadvantage of hope?
It knows how to deceive. (71)[17]

In fact, Malvina's question, according to the game's rules, unlike the questions formulated by other participants, goes beyond a mere demand for explanation or merely giving a name to and juxtaposing universal moral issues. Hardly conforming to the game's sentential poetics, it tugs at the innermost, and at the same time most secret, strings of the asker's and answerer's hearts. It carries a demand to give a name to the power, and not to the essence of one's inner experience.[18] It aims at eliciting a verbal response from Ludomir as a sign of his affective response, feeling, or impression. The response is impossible to convey directly or to observe from the outside, but in Malvina's view it ought to find expression and justification in the inner lives of them both, playing its role without ostentation. Because of its secretive form, written and thus visible only to their eyes, Malvina's question fulfils a protective function with respect to the potential, immaterial, and directly unutterable nature of what is, ultimately, meant to be part of the answer.

Ludomir's involuntary but knowing gestures, made when the question reaches him, are evidence to Malvina that the question has tugged at a sensitive and somewhat problematic heartstring. The answer, in

---

17 In his work on La Rochefoucauld's *Maxims*, Roland Barthes points out that in the maxim's "architecture" a more important role than that of "relations" is played by "formal essences": "usually substantives but occasionally adjectives or verbals as well, each of which refers to a complete, eternal, in fact autarchic meaning: love, passion, pride, wound, deceive, delicate, impatient". Relations "of comparison or of antithesis" are less obvious than their constituents: "in the maxim, the intellect first perceives certain complete substances, not the gradual flux of the thought". Barthes claims that this results from the fact that the maxim's "architecture" is "a substitute for the versified languages", and that "there is [...] a special affinity between verse and maxim, between aphoristic and divinatory communication" (Barthes 1990, 5–6).

18 It might be said, drawing on Barthes' definitions, that Malvina's question transcends the poetics of the aphorism in as much as it turns into a question about an aspect, and not the essence, of Ludomir's experience. It is in that sense that the question may be said to express a progressive "flux of thought". Barthes makes this even more precise: the maxim is, "by the very state of the maxim's structure with a relation of essence not of praxis, of identity, not of transformation" (Barthes 1990, 5).

turn, which faithfully recalls the last word of the question as its first word, and relates directly to the issue raised in this question, confirms Malvina's premonition that her question has touched upon an internal issue, veiled in mystery: "The impression, unfortunately, will never ever be erased. / But merciful kindness should perhaps not remind me of it" (71).[19]

Let us note that the affective value of the word "impression", the key word in this two-dimensional game, is associated with the feeling of unshaken constancy (this is the meaning which seems to arise from Ludomir's declaration) and at the same time with a feeling of unwavering constancy (this meaning is implied by the final question mark to the first sentence of the declaration). Consequently, the affective value of this word becomes related to the confidential sphere, where silence is highly recommended.

The narrator does not provide detailed information about how Malvina understands Ludomir's answer. Her account matches the secrecy of the message which the heroine receives through reading. The reader is only given general information: Malvina has reconfirmed her attitude towards the secrecy of Ludomir's actions and responded with silence and subsequent warming of her affection for him.

The structural mastery of this scene is an extension of the mastery of the entire Warsaw plot. It consists in the fact that although the protagonists' spatial proximity (achieved through the mirror and the game) is transformed into genuine affective closeness, like that experienced earlier at Krzewin (through a return in their conversation and written exchange of ideas to "indirect" communication), and although Malvina seems certain on the basis of this about the personal identity of Ludomir

---

19 It must be noted that Melsztyński-Ludomir's answer is punctuated differently in the 1822 "Third Revised Edition". The first part of Ludomir's answer ends with a question mark, which means that Ludomir replies to Malvina's question with another question. In later, inter-war and post-war, editions, the first question mark is turned into an exclamation mark or replaced with a full-stop. This is also the case with the 1978 edition of *Malvina*. Witold Billip, the editor, writes: "The text of the novel was based on the second edition, Warsaw 1817, having taken account of some minor but telling changes introduced by the author or some authorised person in the third edition, Warsaw 1822" (1978, 30; trans. M.O.). It is only the presence of the question mark at the end of Melsztyński-Ludomir's answer that renders the entire answer precarious enough in terms of meaning, so that its content may refer to the time and the place and the events which Ludomir wishes to keep secret (Krzewin), or the time, the place and the events which Prince Melsztyński wishes to keep secret (the Florynka affair). Turning the beginning of the answer into an exclamation or a statement relates it unambiguously to Ludomir's secrets, while the game itself is far from unambiguous.

Prince Melsztyński, these salon exchanges of "secret codes" could hardly be more error-ridden. In effect, Malvina is never further from solving the riddle than at that particular moment.

This whole scene is an exact reversal of the protagonists' first Warsaw meeting. It fills the emotional void which stretches between Malvina and her beloved. The differences between the form of his and her utterances, which Malvina had previously observed and responded to negatively, disappear. The opposition between Malvina's epistolary utterance and Ludomir's speech, alongside the speech of others around him, no longer persists. Suddenly, whatever has so far remained separate now becomes united. Firstly, this pertains to Malvina's and her beloved's thoughts and feelings. Secondly, not only the most intimate content communicated by them to each other, both through speech and through writing, but also the manner of formulating and articulating these utterances, defines them as bearers of "secret messages". And last but not least, these spoken-aloud and written utterances, normally dissimilar and disconnected, resonate, in this one and only situation, with each other in form, content and even space, "speaking" with one and the same language of shared experiences and affective stirrings, as they did at Krzewin. In Warsaw, however, they are translated at one time into the language of conversational metaphors, and at another – into playful aphorisms.

What coexists jointly, however, to the point of achieving unity in this scene, as the scene closes as well as in the immediately following sequences of events, exists only as psychologically disjointed, both formally and spatially. The ever-changing emotional stance of the heroine's beloved, demonstrated in his utterances and in the discrepancy between the formal properties of these utterances, is embodied, as far as Malvina is concerned, in two different figures of Ludomir. One represents inner perfection; the other – playfulness, spite and mockery, which the narrator labels "vanity of habits" (85) or "licentiousness" (111). Again, the reciprocation of both protagonists' concealed experiences, whose foundation are the reality, events and symbols known only to them, manifests itself exclusively through their conflictive behaviour rather than through concurrences in their spoken and written exchanges. These include conflicts between what both communicate in their own conversations (and what other characters say about them), and what Malvina herself writes in her letters (alongside what others write about the two of them). The account which directly follows the scene opens with the narrator's reference to the rift in the protagonists' mental unity:

But, alas, what should have come to Ludomir's aid constantly turned against him, as though some malevolent fate sought a means to distance and separate them. Malvina's friendlier treatment of him had restored his hopes and good humour but had also restored him at the same time to his customary manner, to the mood in which Malvina had so far seen him in Warsaw and which seemed so different from his disposition at Krzewin. He began to talk too much, to debate out loud, to make fun of everyone and everything. (72)

Heart and Thoughts

Plotting the Warsaw events around Malvina and Ludomir's participation in a salon game which consists in a written exchange of aphoristic questions and answers, is both curious and extraordinary. Equally curious and extraordinary is the presentation of this exchange as Malvina's early response to the disintegration of Ludomir's speech into sound and meaning. Let me now return to more general aspects, both historical and theoretical, signalled in the first part of this study. These revolve around issues related to intonation and gesture, raised by Rousseau and Herder. One issue, discussed by Rousseau, were the roles of intonation and "mute eloquence" of gestures (1998, 29) in giving speech "sentiment and truth" (1979, 72), as counterparts to otherness and falsehood, which intonation and gestures may also convey. The second issue, raised by Herder, was the ambiguity of intonations and gestures as elements of speech when expressed through writing, where they "represent" live voices and gestures.

Malvina's confusion, due to the disintegration of Ludomir's speech into sound and meaning, as well as her uncertainty prompted by the changing meanings of his writing, point to the very essence of the issues pondered by Rousseau and Herder. The sources of Malvina's first reaction, just like the reflections of both these thinkers, may be sought in the very sensitivity to disruption in the emotional and moral expression of speech that ought after all to reflect the speakers' sincerity. The shared basis for Malvina's second response and Rousseau and Herder's discussions is their sensitivity to the nature of the dilemma faced by the heart and the thoughts, when these cognitive faculties are forced to determine the "sentiment and truth" contained in written, and not spoken, utterances. This is what interests us here the most. We need to re-examine the circumstances which attend Malvina's response to Ludomir's written communications. We also need to shift the weight of our analysis to these crucial issues, which pertain to the different roles played by speech and writing in reflecting human inner lives, and consequently – in shaping human relationships. These fundamental issues form the basis of those already discussed, and concern the intonational and gesticulatory validation of speech. They also are the basis of the concurrence between Malvina's first response and the arguments of the two philosophers. More specific issues were contemplated in Rousseau's *Émile*, while the fundamental ones were discussed in his *L'Essai sur l'origine des langues*.[20] Herder's "Treatise on the Origin of Language", in turn, covers both sets of issues in connection with both speech and writing.

Let us return once again to the recently discussed sequence of events. By placing Malvina and Ludomir in a contractual situation, the game of *secrétaire* creates favourable conditions in which the written sentential messages passed between them may be turned into manifestations of secret codes, otherwise uncommunicable. The fact that the messages are not uttered "directly" does not seem to disturb the protagonists' expression and comprehension of the communications. On the contrary, making connections with their past exchanges seems to guarantee the success of both expression and comprehension. But precisely where the written statements lose their directness and become the loci for secret communications, they are affected by a disintegration in meaning. They embarrass the hero and disorient the heroine. This occurs as if the messages did not derive from one objective and did not serve one goal, as if they had not turned into a secret exchange. The heroine now faces the question of what is amiss: is it the authenticity of the affection manifested by Ludomir, or perhaps her attempts at comprehending those manifestations?

---

20 I am aware of three discussions of the issues raised in Rousseau's *L'Essai sur l'origine des langues*: by Jacques Derrida (1967), Maria R. Mayenowa (1970) and Angèle Kremer-Marietti (1974). Derrida's remarks in *Of Grammatology* are directly pertinent to the aspects of speech and writing pondered by Rousseau, and most interesting to me here. I have decided, however, when elucidating Rousseau's standpoint on these issues, to follow not Derrida, but Mayenowa. Derrida is fascinated not only by Rousseau's view on the relation between speech and writing, but also by its reversal, i.e. putting into question Rousseau's main assumption that "[l]anguages are made to be spoken, writing is nothing but a *supplement* of speech" (Derrida 1997, 295; italics original). In simultaneous agreement and disagreement with Rousseau, Derrida formulates the notion of writing as present "before speech and in speech" (1997, 51), and more generally – constructs the idea of a science of writing, i.e. *grammatology* (1997, 51; 76). The foundation for this concept of writing and proposed science of writing is a specifically conceived notion of the trace, as synonymous with *différance*, from which meaning originates (Derrida 1997, 65). But because my objective is, above all, to offer a faithful overview of Rousseau's main ideas concerning speech and writing, I will follow Mayenowa rather than Derrida, although I support Derrida's views for a number of other reasons. As for Kremer-Marietti, she touches upon Derrida's main points, but refrains from problematizing them.

Is it Ludomir's heart which does not manifest itself in his speech, or is it her own thoughts which fail to detect his heart in his speech? Her heart checks the cognitive acts of her thoughts, and vice versa. Malvina's eyes, which glance at Ludomir and then at the text of his sentential utterance, illustrate these criss-crossing actions.

According to Rousseau, among the phenomena that from time immemorial have shaped human relationships, writing is distinctly different from speech, even though it is the visual equivalent of speech and provides additional cognitive values to those provided by speech. In Rousseau's view, writing is considered a tool with which to discipline human linguistic expression into intellectual accuracy. In contrast, speech is a tool which gives emotional intensity to that expression. Rousseau sees the distinctive features of writing in the exchange of thoughts, and distinctive features of speech in the exchange of emotions. The merits of writing and written communications are not viewed by Rousseau as natural. He assesses them through the loss which they inflict on the merits of human speech, but also through what differentiates these two kinds of merit. Here is what Rousseau himself says on the subject:

> Writing, which seems as if it should fix language, is precisely what alters it; it changes not its words but its genius; it substitutes precision for expressiveness. Feelings are conveyed when one speaks and ideas when one writes. In writing, one is forced to take all the words according to common acceptation; but he who speaks varies the meanings by the tone of his voice, he determines them as he pleases; less constrained to be clear, he grants more to forcefulness, and it is not possible for a language one writes to keep for long the liveliness of one that is only spoken. Words are written and not sounds: now, in an accented language it is the sounds, the accents, the inflections of every sort that constitute the greatest energy of the language; and that make a turn of phrase, even a common one, belong only in the place it is found. (1998, 300)

In order for the written exchange between Malvina and Ludomir's sentential questions and answers to recreate the liveliness and fullness of understanding experienced in their past conversations, it would have to bring joy to their hearts and fill their thoughts at the same time. In other words, it would have to be perceived by the interlocutors as eagerly awaited, fitting and accurate in every word and every sense, while concealing its intended message. This would mean that a silent game of writing and speech had taken place within the exchange, enabling the emergence of the questions and answers as a genuinely informal and secret dialogue, "belong[ing] only in the place it is found" (Rousseau 1998, 300). This would then mean that the very properties of written questions and answers, complemented and secured with punctuation, had successfully entered the role of the voice signs that had earlier nuanced their former conversations, the "sounds, the accents, the inflections of every sort" (Rousseau 1998, 300). Meanwhile, as I have shown, this possibility has been squandered. The written exchange of sentential messages "paralyses" the protagonists. The inconstancy of Ludomir's speech (from Malvina's viewpoint) and Malvina's unfriendly message (from Ludomir's viewpoint) contradict not only the thoughts, but also the hearts of the protagonists.

Rousseau's stance on the differences between speech and writing, which highlights a preference for thoughts rather than feelings in writing, has its origins in his high regard for the voice and feeling as the material and psychological foundations of language communication. In his view, it is not needs but feelings that stimulate humans to influence one another by means of language. By "feelings", he means inner experiences which cannot remain unexpressed, and which open up or close certain individuals to others, creating either sympathy or estrangement between them. All this is expressed by speech. It is speech, and not writing, according to Rousseau, that takes precedence in this task. This is because natural components, such as voice-modulated sounds, stresses and intonations, are present in speech signs. In the voice, viewed as potential sign matter, without carrying any specific utterance, Rousseau sees an instrument capable of effecting closeness between people. When comparing the most commonly used kinds of communicative sign matter, he declares: "Colors are the finery of inanimate beings; all matter is colored; but sounds proclaim movement, the voice proclaims a sensitive being" (Rousseau 1998, 325). It is no coincidence then that in the intonation which he describes as the voiced modulation of the meaning of an utterance, he sees an instrument capable of reflecting either the speakers' moral integrity or their departures from it.

According to Rousseau, conventional graphic signs are capable, as he puts it, of stressing the paradoxical aspect of this, of "depict[ing] sounds and speak[ing] to the eyes" (Rousseau 1998, 297). In the development of historical forms of writing, in the transformations of the "manners of writing" until "alphabetic writing" emerged, he sees a gradual reduction of this natural, object-based factor in favour of the conventional and sign-based. The process, he tells us, has comprised three key stages: "The first manner of writing is not to depict sounds but the objects themselves, whether directly as the Mexicans did, or by allegorical figures as the

Egyptians did of old" (Rousseau 1998, 297); "to represent words and propositions by conventional characters" (Rousseau 1998, 297), which was typical of Chinese writing; or to "break down the speaking voice into a certain number of elementary parts, whether vowels or articulations, with which one could form all imaginable words and syllables" (Rousseau 1998, 297), the latter being the source of origin of our alphabetic writing. The essence of relations which began to connect speech and alphabetic writing is thus epitomised by Rousseau: "This is not precisely to depict speech, it is to analyze it" (1998, 297).

Let me once again return to Malvina's dilemma. I would like to consider some related questions, alongside those reflected in Rousseau's views on intonation, from the vantage point of later formulations by J. L. Austin, which have drawn the attention of linguists to the utterance as a speech act.[21] They would seem to be concurrent. Naturally, this concerns only the concurrence of the types of questions and issues, and not their particular formulations. This concurrence matters, on the one hand, because the questions expressing the essence of Malvina's dilemma are linked to the issue of "truthfulness" of speech as carrier of feeling, hence – to the "interpretation" of speech. On the other hand, Austin – when trying to pinpoint the way in which speech carries meaning, moves around a set of notions that relate to the physical (voice-related), conventional (meaning-related), spiritual and moral (ethical) components of speech. It is impossible not to see Austin's dilemma as identical to that of Rousseau, and of Malvina:

> But we are apt to have a feeling that [the words] being serious consists in their being uttered as (merely) the outward and visible sign, for convenience or other record or for information, of an inward and spiritual act: from which it is but a short step to go on to believe or to assume without realizing that for many purposes the outward utterance is a description, true or false, of the occurrence of the inward performance. The classic expression of this idea is to be found in the Hippolytus (l. 612), where Hippolytus says: "my tongue swore to, but my heart (or mind or other backstage artiste) did not". Thus "I promise to..." obliges me – puts on record my spiritual assumption of a spiritual shackle.
>
> It is gratifying to observe in this very example how excess of profundity, or rather solemnity, at once paves the way for immortality. For one who says

---

21 While drawing on J. L. Austin's *How to do Things with Words*, I do not intend to present, much less interpret, Austin's theory. I only refer to one of its threads, touching upon its major issue: the representation of an utterance as an illocutionary act.

"promising is not merely a matter of uttering words! It is an inward and spiritual act!" is apt to appear as a solid moralist standing out against a generation of superficial theorizers: we see him as he sees himself, surveying the invisible depths of ethical space, with all the distinction of a specialist in the *sui generis*. Yet he provides Hippolytus with a let-out, the bigamist with an excuse for his "I do" and the welsher with a defence for his "I bet". Accuracy and morality alike are on the side of the plain saying that *our word is our bond*. (Austin 1962, 9–10; italics original)

In this passage, Austin's arguments are polemical. He defends the assumption that the words with which we promise or bet "inasmuch as" in "the depths of ethical space" (Austin 1962, 10) conceal our moral obligation. At the same time, while opposing "solid moralists", Austin also stresses the significance of the psychological and moral components of a spoken utterance (1962, 10). This is why his arguments help us to understand that Malvina's dilemma consists in eliminating the uncertainties surrounding the discrepancy between the two aspects of Ludomir's utterance, the verbal and that contained in "the invisible depths of ethical space" (Austin 1962, 10). They also help us to see Malvina's dilemma as a reading, by the heart and by the thoughts, of the heart's "pledge" and of the signs of the spoken utterance.

These findings bring me to the following reflections. It is the task of those who depict the "feelings", "errors" or "passions" of Hippolytus or Malvina to expose the invisible conflicts resulting from these characters' attitudes towards the non-transparency of utterances, whether their own or other people's. This writerly task involves another. It is the task of philosophers and theoreticians of language to stress that the utterance, whether of Hippolytus, Malvina or anyone else, because of its non-transparent sign-related nature, cannot be reduced either to a spiritual act (an inner, spiritual, fictional whole, which could only be manifested in words), or to a phonetic act (the physical minimum). In a word, it is their task to demonstrate that the most distinctive feature of an utterance is that the utterance itself is an act of creating meaning, i.e. of performing through speech and accentuating the ways in which the words should be understood at any given moment. This distinctive feature of an utterance, whose "other side" is revealed by writers, and whose essence – by philosophers and theoreticians of language, imposes on Hippolytus, Malvina and anyone else the fixed role of originators and interpreters of the non-transparency of utterances.

The arguments of both Rousseau and Austin have convinced me that Malvina's dilemma has been, and still is, no trivial issue. As a factor which complicates the Warsaw plot, it contributes to the development of a typical Enlightenment motif: the "ambiguity" of the human world (Barthes 1990, 15). At the same time, it carries typically romantic content, i.e. the ambiguity is invaded by utterances that have been individually formulated, emotionally or indeed subconsciously experienced, both spoken-aloud (externalised) and unspoken (not allowed to be externalised).

The Letter as Carrier of Suppressed or Publicized Words[22]

As the Warsaw plot unfolds, the protagonists' mental, emotional and utterance-related disconnection is gradually clarified. Malvina's turning again towards the discrepancies between the contradictory or doppelgänger incarnations of Ludomir arranges the meanings potentially hidden within his sentential reply to her sentential question into layers. In other words, the final phase of the Warsaw plot, the clarification of earlier events after later ones have occurred, including Malvina's already mentioned experience of Ludomir's personal non-identity in an atmosphere typical of the use of the doppelgänger motif, all suggest that the exchange of sentential messages could have combined the meanings related to the two different spheres of the protagonists' experiences. In short, the essence of Ludomir's reply might have misleadingly corresponded to the essence of Malvina's question, and thus erroneously confirmed his personal identity.

Let us note that the presentation of the episodes in the mirrored conversation and the game of *secrétaire* as misleading in the riddle-solving process has its origin in the ending of both episodes. After all, Ludomir's reply is so disorientating that Malvina cannot be certain that the essence of her question was, for him, concealed in the place name "Krzewin":

Did not last summer, did not last August
leave any lasting impression?
[...]

---

22 Here I draw on Gottfried Wilhelm Leibniz's idea that a letter is a "carrier" of words (1996, 137).

The impression, unfortunately, will never ever be erased.
But merciful kindness should perhaps not remind me of it. (71)

From Malvina's viewpoint, the expressive quality of "unfortunately" is too ambiguous to be interpreted as reinforcing the sense of unwavering constancy, which could have sounded to Malvina like a confession, or more likely – a statement of failure, related to a confusing sense of unwavering constancy. Last but not least, the questioning quality of his reply in fact erases its declarative message, which might have confirmed the expectation contained in Malvina's question. Consequently, it is not the further course of events but the very finales of both amorous episodes that makes Malvina realise the existence not of one shared experience but of two disparate spheres of events, in which the two of them have located their secret experiences.

A complete division into layers, and the resulting separation of meanings linked by the question-and-answer exchange, occurs in the sequence of events centred around Alfred's letter, read aloud by Lissowski in the salon. The key scene in this sequence is a reversal of the preceding one, which features the conversation and game of *secrétaire*. In the latter, the written messages turn other characters into mutes, as the questions and answers are read only by participants in the game. Now, in Lissowski's reading, the written message can be heard by all those present. In the former, written messages express the lovers' quintessential secrets. Now, they serve to publicize these secrets. It is the powerful contrast between, on the one hand, the events recounted by Alfred in his letter and the use Lissowski makes of them, and on the other – the affection itself and the idea of affection which Malvina cherishes and upholds, that ultimately separate the meanings of the lovers' exchanges in the game. Hence Ludomir's statement turns into a message which results from his temporary expiation for having embraced the "inferior", "licentious" aspect of relationships, in which two people are not bound by the imperative of fidelity. It does not result from any intention to assure Malvina of his unwavering support for the "superior", ideal aspect of a relationship.

I shall now point to the main structural and thematic motifs in the scene depicting the response of the audience to Lissowski's reading aloud of Alfred's letter. The letter itself has already been quoted in full.

Lissowski, following his plan to introduce discord between Malvina and Ludomir, skilfully kindles the salon community's interest in the letter which is in his possession. First, when the conversation turns to Ludomir's departure, Lissowski "mention[s] Alfred's letter" (110); next, when the interest intensifies, he "produc[es] the letter from his pocket" (110), saying that Alfred "has seen Ludomir and even brings me an amusing anecdote about him" (110); and finally, on the audience's request that he "show" the letter (111), he begins to read the letter aloud. Malvina's discomposure (the tea spilling incident), visible to the company and occasioned by Lissowski's actions, precedes the disappointment which she experiences inwardly ("distress" and "a dismal impression", 111) because of the events of which she learns as the letter is read aloud.

Lissowski's act testifies to his in-depth understanding of the practices and conventions used to circulate publicly half-confidential and half-gossipy information. After all, Alfred's letter is a means of circulating opinions about people and events ("Perhaps you will be able to piece together from this story a nice bit of tittle-tattle that will assist you in your courtship of the angelic Malvina, blackening Ludomir a little in her eyes", 110). The use that Lissowski makes of the letter is aimed at showing Ludomir in an ambiguous light. Malvina's anxiety, in turn, implies a fear of making public that part of her life in which Ludomir's ambiguity features as an issue in its own right, one which Malvina only reveals in letters. That is why she almost becomes the heroine of a "scene" which "might have attracted all eyes towards Malvina" (111). After all, Alfred's letter discusses with piquancy and cynicism the events which link Ludomir to a young woman called Florynka, emphasising the love affair and the yet inexplicable "telling" details. Lissowski's initiative acts as a foil to Malvina's inner love life. And the letter which he reads is a foil to the secrecy of her epistolary communications. This is suggested by the heroine's inner experiences, as the narrator tells us. The most important part in them is played by her disillusioned recollections. Her acknowledgement of Ludomir's unfaithfulness to her after the Krzewin days replaces the imagery of perfect love and human virtue, so far symbolised to her by this locality:

She recalled with tearful wretchedness the previous summer and the happy days at Krzewin, when she would have been unable to conceive of Ludomir ever being fond of anyone but herself. Alas! Almost every passing day (since Malvina had made her entry into high society) bore away with it one of the thousands of delusions which, in her lonely youth, she had imagined to be so entrancing and which at Krzewin had seemed to have come true in Ludomir's heart. (111)

Ambiguity of the Human World

The masterly co-ordination of the spoken and written turns in the narrative with the complications in the Warsaw plot enables Wirtemberska to reflect in it a whole range of inter-related issues. Put in the most general terms, it can be said that the Warsaw plot demonstrates Ludomir's dual personality against a backdrop of the more general ambiguity of human personalities, faces, deeds and utterances (the mystery of Ludomir and the theatricality of the salon). If we wish, however, to capture the essence of this issue, it should be stated that the Warsaw plot demonstrates both the excellent adjustment by some characters to the dictates of ambiguity and the experience of ambiguity as torment (Lissowski and Doryda openly parade their preference for theatrical "polite hypocrisy"; Malvina shows "cold politeness" towards theatrical behaviours outwardly, but inwardly they make her feel confused and helpless). Below are passages from letters by Lissowski and by Malvina, written roughly at the same time:

> Lissowski: "We are beginning to play out a comedy in which Ludomir, Malvina, Doryda and your humble servant will be playing the principal roles. Confidants and soubrettes are to be found for the asking! (the Sheriff is already a ready-made confidant). Who will be the best actor and how the drama's plot will unravel, we will learn shortly". (61)

> Malvina: "My Wanda! Now I know who he is, this strange, this mysterious Ludomir... or rather I don't know, I don't understand, I cannot comprehend anything that touches upon his fate or his conduct!" (59)[23]

That is not all: the Warsaw plot enables us to perceive that experiencing the duality of what is seen and what is heard as something unbearable that we might wish to control, implies the unending differentiation, separation and selection for ourselves of the possible meanings of the faces, characters, deeds, and primarily – utterances that we encounter. This is shown in the unspoken disapproval of Ludomir's character, formulated by Malvina in her thoughts and letters, thereby making him a representative of theatrical "polite hypocrisy". Moreover, the plot suggests that in this way the meanings of certain phenomena are given ethical preference over others. This may be seen in those situations where

---

23 The theatre, and more precisely – acting, is one of the most common metaphors used to signify the ambiguity of the human world.

Malvina's mental and epistolary acknowledgment of Ludomir's positive traits is accompanied by her conviction that theirs is a perfect love, an idealisation ascribed by one of the partners to the other, which sustains the affective commitment.

It is thus impossible not to view *Malvina* as a novel which combines two broad topics running through the culture of the European Enlightenment. One is the non-transparency of the human world: the appearance of "masks, veils and paint" (Barthes 1990, 15) on faces, in characters, in their deeds and utterances, when the values or intentions indicated by means of such phenomena are lacking, or when others make themselves known. The other is the non-transparency of speech: its ambiguities which keep the speakers in a state of uncertainty and can lead either to complete comprehension, or to errors and misunderstandings.[24]

The fact that in *Malvina* both topics come to interact in the Warsaw plot, set in the salon and around it, corroborates a profound cultural pattern. The tradition of French seventeenth- and eighteenth-century salons, and in particular – the forms of social life which they cultivated and which gave inspiration to Wirtemberska's Warsaw salon, centred around their interaction. The former topic was, however, essentially located within the domain of literature, while the latter – within philosophical reflection on language. In order to demonstrate how far the salon combines these two large topics, the moral and the linguistic, let me recall two scholars and their considerations.

On the one hand, there is the argument of Roland Barthes that the question of "How to read man?" (1990, 15) ran through the works of Racine and La Rochefoucauld as much as it did through the texts produced by salon attendees. On the other hand, it should be noted, following Zofia Florczak, that the essence of contemporary reflection on language consisted in judgments about the meaning of words, particularly those connoting moral notions, "which could not be specified by pointing to a tangible correlative" (1978, 30; trans. M.O.). When reading the longish passage by Barthes about La Rochefoucauld's *Maxims* (further below), let us keep in mind the fragment from Leibniz's meditation on moral reasons, which in his view constitute, coincidentally, one of the formal criteria for the origin of the meanings of words:

I know that the Scholastics and everyone else are given to saying that the significations of words are arbitrary (*ex insituto*), and it is true that they are

---

24   The major aspects of this issue are discussed by Teresa Kostkiewiczowa (1990).

not settled by natural necessity, but they are settled by reasons – sometimes natural ones in which chance plays some part, sometimes moral ones which involve choice. (1990, 279)

These statements from Leibniz come from his polemic with John Locke on the then topical debate on the nature of linguistic signs, and form an inseparable component of theories of language developed by Rousseau, Herder, and others. Florczak writes:

Both Locke and Leibniz raised as very important the problem of "names", i.e. word meanings. They were interested in the origins of names, their semantic transformations (from the concrete, perceived by the senses, to the general and abstract), the possibilities for defining names or elucidating their meanings, and consequently, in the issue of word unambiguity. (1978, 108; trans. M.O.)

The categories which Leibniz uses to describe the origins of word meanings are developed by Barthes as he elaborates on La Rochefoucauld's *Maxims*. The *Maxims* reflect the sarcasm of a salon frequenter who derives no self-assurance from moral notions that require demystifying specifications of "how many" and "what kind of" properties define their essence. The *Maxims* first and foremost attack concepts of virtues based on popular meanings of moral notions, typically conceived of and applied without reflection. The maxims give names to the less noble aspects of deeds, qualities and values, usually concealed behind their nobler sides, such as vanity, weakness, *amour propre*, laziness and, primarily, self-love. Let us remember that self-love ("vanity" in the English translation) is the subject of the very first sentence of Wirtemberska's preface to *Malvina*. Let us also remember that both in her preface and novel itself, virtues are viewed as unattainable ideals which have the power nevertheless to channel human activity and sensibility. It is interesting that Barthes's reconstructive depiction of the maxim includes an analysis of its mythical context, updated in the combination of linguistic and moral issues in the maxim and in its home environment, i.e. the salon:

The maxim is a two-faced being, here tragic, there bourgeois; despite its austere stamp, its stinging and pure writing, it is essentially an ambiguous discourse, located on the frontier of two worlds. Which ones? We can say, that of death and that of play. On death's side, we have the tragic question *par excellence*, addressed by man to the silent god: *Who am I?* This is the question ceaselessly formulated by the Racinian hero, Eriphyle, for instance, who keeps trying to know herself and who dies of the effort; this is also the question of the *Maxims*: it is answered by the terrible, the funereal is only of restrictive identity, and again, as we have seen, this answer itself is uncertain, since man never definitively abandons the dream of virtue. But this mortal question is also, *par excellence*, the question of every form of play. Interrogating Oedipus as to the nature of man, the Sphinx established both tragic discourse and ludic discourse, the game of death (since for Oedipus the wages of ignorance was death) and the game of the salon. *Who are you?* This riddle is also the question of the *Maxims*; as we have seen, everything, in their structure, is very close to a verbal game, not, of course, to a chance conflagration of words as the surrealists might conceive it – they too, moreover, great maxim-makers – but at least to a submission of meaning to certain pre-established forms, as if the formal rule were an instrument of truth. We know that La Rochefoucauld's maxims are, in fact, a product of salon games (portraits, riddles, sentences); and this encounter of the tragic and the worldly, one grazing the other, is not the least of the truths which the *Maxims* propose for us. (Barthes 1990, 21–22; italics original)

At the salon of Marquise de Rambouillet, the prototype of eighteenth- and nineteenth-century salons, La Rochefoucauld was a star of the first magnitude. I have juxtaposed passages from Leibniz and Barthes in order to illustrate the extent to which the circle of Marquise de Rambouillet and the greatest philosophers of the day shared the same interests. By doing so, I also expect to show how far Princess Wirtemberska (at this point I use her aristocratic title on purpose), by using the cultural context of the salon (but not the literary salon) and the mechanism of *secrétaire* in her novel's plot, situated herself within the field of earlier, seventeenth-century linguistic and moral issues. She used it and drew on it, however, in an innovative, pre-romantic spirit. At this stage, I do not intend to go into issues related to the salons of Marquise de Rambouillet and Princess Wirtemberska because this will be one of the subjects discussed in the final, fourth part of this study. Let me repeat only the most important factual information after Alina Aleksandrowicz (1974). Wirtemberska's salon, in terms of its internal organisation and the style of literary and social activities pursued in it, imitated the salon of Marquise de Rambouillet. As in that Parisian salon, among the intellectual pastimes which attracted artists, writers and politicians, word and discussion games were popular, as was practical study of language. Wirtemberska's salon throve on the study of synonyms, which in the eighteenth century were a favourite with salon attendees and linguists alike. They were one of the recurrent issues in the debate on the nature of primeval human language. Zbigniew Kloch, author of a study on the growing interest in synonyms in Poland at the turn of the nineteenth century (1993), labels the creative practices developed in connection with them in Wirtemberska's salon "the synonymy game".

It is time to move on to Wirtemberska's pioneering, pre-romantic views on eighteenth-century linguistic and moral issues centred around the "ambiguity" of the human world. This is clearly illustrated by two components, or – in other words – two particular characteristics of the novel. One is Malvina's way of experiencing Ludomir's non-transparent speech, different faces and characters as well as those of people around him. Pervaded by her personal reasoning skills (symbolised by a mental capacity referred to as "intuiting", or more directly – as "intuition"), as well as by her emotionality which prevents her from using those skills, it leads her not only into error, but also towards almost perfect foreknowledge (this psychological capacity is in turn symbolised by the word "heart"). The other pre-romantic particular is the reflection on the links between love and happiness, indulged in by the narrator as the situation of Malvina and Ludomir shifts from positive to negative. In one such reflection, included – importantly – still in the positive period, she expresses the belief that happiness cannot exist without satisfying one's preoccupation with the "thoughts, soul, heart" of "the beloved creature" (31):

> It is a fortunate thing in life to be loved. But I would add that it is already a fortunate thing to love, that being in love perhaps even surpasses being loved.
>
> When one is very much in love, one's thoughts, soul, heart are occupied with this alone. No hour is indifferent. The days are filled most pleasantly with this one preoccupation, with the single thought of how to delight and enhance the destiny of the beloved creature, not only in important but also in the most trivial situations. (31)

Afterwards, when Malvina's non-reciprocation comes to the fore, as a result of the mysterious transformation of Ludomir, the narrator high-lights the constant activity of her "thoughts, soul, heart" (31) as well as their orientation towards the unknown.

From our present vantage point, which is to illustrate Wirtember-ska's novel's pre-romantic approach to linguistic and moral issues as they relate to the seventeenth-century "ambiguity" of the human world (Barthes 1990, 15), even the fact that Malvina's experiences are plotted along two different but interacting lines seems less important: the situational (in and around the salon) and the mental (in her letters). From this perspective, what matters most is that, in Malvina's experience, along both interacting lines, her selection of the meaning of Ludomir's speech, face or character, is a knot of inseparably interwoven thinking and loving "skills" (symbolised by the eponymous cognitive and moral category of "the heart's intuition"). Moreover, the narrator interprets her choice in the spirit of the ethics of love and happiness, based on, as we would put it today, a combination of rational and instinctive mental effort when facing the unknown, indefinite, "other" side of another human being's speech, face and character.

Over many decades, between Locke and Leibniz, and Rousseau and Herder, between Marquise de Rambouillet and Princess Wirtemberska, a distinct shift occurred in the interests of philosophers and writers: from the cognitive and instrumental functions of language to the creative and ornamental. And although meaning remained a major issue, the way in which it was understood changed, too: it ceased to be exclusively an issue of notional ideas, analogous to the processes taking place in the human mind. It became as much a matter of signs of mental states, an expression of a more holistically conceived human being. Representations of such transformations, as depicted by Zofia Florczak or by Paul Ricoeur, supplement one another. There is much to suggest that the particularities of style and the problematics of *Malvina* span the extremes of these very transformations. Language and meaning are understood as substitutes for mental processes too generalised to be individuated, but also their opposite, i.e. the understanding and presentation of these phenomena in a way individuated enough for them to also figure as substitutes for emotion. The formal characteristics and problematics of *Malvina* are saturated, as I have tried to demonstrate, with the characteristics and content of both cultural orders of understanding language and meaning. One is the classical, of which the author of *Malvina* was a continuator, the other – was the romantic, of which she was a pioneer on Polish soil. European literary salons were institutions in which these transformations called into being new varieties of personal lifestyle and new forms of literary style. This is why the most frequently observed (but barely studied) features of *Malvina*, such as its Sentimentalism, Sterneism, Ossianism, legacy of Delille, or its borrowing from the then popular Madame Cottin, ought to be viewed as topics endowed with their own language and meaning indicators, which inhabit the space created by the correspondences and oppositions between language and meaning derived from the novel's classical and romantic features.[25]

Twins, Affection and Marriage

In its discussion of issues of the world's non-transparency and of language, Wirtemberska's novel displays one more distinguishing feature which, like those already discussed, is indicative of a more profound cultural pattern. Here I mean a motif which is conspicuous throughout the entire plot, but becomes particularly striking in its final sections, when it ceases to be merely the subject of the central riddle and turns into the solution to that riddle. It consists in the duality of the characters participating in the plot: two sisters, Malvina and Wanda; and two brothers, Ludomir and Prince Melsztyński. The latter two, when the riddle is finally solved, are found to be look-alikes because they are twins. More precisely, the duality of similarities and differences in physical and personality traits in both pairs of siblings illustrates, as a result of their complicated genealogies, two different cases of personal unity in duality and, at the same time, personal duality in unity.

The most important components of the Warsaw plot are masterfully linked to this co-existence of unity and duality within the character pairs of two sisters and two twin brothers. The link pertains both to the split of Ludomir's person into two, discussed by Malvina in her letters to her sister, which confirms his salon transformation and denies it at the same time, and to his salon companions pretending to be people who they are not, which Malvina also perceives. We should not forget that in the interplay of consequences resulting from the conflicts between unity and duality inscribed in family relations, as well as in the theatricality of the characters' actions, one more conflict of this kind surfaces. It is the break-up of the emotional bond between Malvina and Ludomir, a woman and a man. As we remember, she fails to keep up with his affective inconstancy, and he – with her constancy. And although the stake in the game between them is to re-establish the quality of their Krzewin affection – with its "truth" (185), "constancy" (191) and "extraordinariness" (182),

---

25 Among all these features of *Malvina,* scholars have been most interested in Sentimentalism and borrowings from Madame Cottin. Both of these are discussed by Juliusz Kleiner (1925). Correspondences between Cottin and Wirtemberska receive a thorough discussion in Budzyk's "Dwie Malwiny" (1966a).

because it is only they who can make their relationship once again a symbol of personal unity, the course of events offers only appearances of the desired state. In other words, the relationship offers merely an affection which falls somewhere on the boundary between truth and falsehood. This feeling fails to turn into the affection which had created the bond between the protagonists in the past. It negates its inner essence, i.e. the fact that it was earlier made real by Malvina and Ludomir, as a symbol of eliminating personal duality. In this way, this feeling plays the role of a counter-symbol by embodying moral ambiguity, which sanctions the protagonists' actual personal duality.

Essentially, then, among the events of the Warsaw part of the plot, including the characters' actions, utterances and experiences, there are none in which personal and moral unity and unambiguity would not clash with personal and moral duality and ambiguity. This leaves a mark on all the characters' relationships in this section of the plot. It affects family relationships, social relationships, as well as those most personal ones which are only just beginning. The multiple forms taken by this game and its subsequent ubiquity were recognised by the creator of the engravings used to illustrate early editions of the novel.[26]

One of these illustrations depicts the central event of the Warsaw plot. It shows the two protagonists looking into the mirror. Caught up

---

26 The illustrations first appeared in the second edition of *Malvina*. There are six of them. They were engraved in France by Jacques Louis Lecerf. Below each are words taken from the novel, which serve to connect the visual representations with the novelistic events. These illustrations receive a general discussion in Zdzisław Libera's "Le problème de l'illustration dans le roman sentimental polonais au début du XIX siècle" (1982). The most striking illustration is subtitled: "She walked up to the mirror". These are the words that begin the narrator's account of the events which cause Malvina's feelings to range between her experiences of her beloved's personal unity and personal duality. The illustrator thus stresses the "mirrored" duality of the heroine's experience. It is hard to know whether, by so doing, Lecerf chooses to interpret this experience in the spirit of Vermeer or of the School of Fontainebleau. The mirror is central to this illustration since it reflects images of the novel's protagonists appearing in front of it, thereby pointing to the former painting tradition. Yet the background presentation of the two rooms, the paired items of furniture and crockery, and most importantly – the portrait of two women and a statuette of two dancers, all point to the latter. According to Michel Foucault, in Dutch painting, mirrors functioned as duplicators by reflecting whatever was in front of them, "only inside an unreal, modified, contracted, concave space" (2002, 8). Mirrors thus represented what had already been presented in the painting, but shaped it differently. The School of Fontainebleau, in turn, favoured metaphorical references between foreground and background scenes. One of the best-known examples is "Le Double Portrait de Gabrielle d'Estrées et de la Duchesse de Villars by an unknown painter". It shows a remarkable spectacle of dualities, at times centred around the "portrait" of two women, at others – of one (Schefer 1969).

in undifferentiated mirror-reflection reciprocity, they are at the same time split into two. From a sideways, somewhat shortened perspective, we see Malvina opposite another Malvina, and Ludomir opposite another Ludomir, and at the same time Malvina and Ludomir opposite another Malvina and Ludomir. Whatever else this illustration shows, apart from this scene, is likewise tinged with duality, although not in the same way as the mirror reflection represents the split into duality. We see two rooms: one in which the mirror spectacle is being enacted, and another one – through an open door. The room with the mirror also features two additional pictures, one of which – in full view – shows two women looking at each other; two ornaments, of which the more visible is a statuette possibly depicting two ballet dancers; as well as duplicated items, which are or are not alike, such as two armchairs and two chandeliers.

Visual art uses means other than verbal to illustrate the wrestling of unity and unambiguity with duality and ambiguity. This pertains to all aspects of the protagonists' relationships that form the subject matter of the Warsaw plot, both in personal and in moral terms. The game is not brought to a close until the riddle of Ludomir's obscured identity is resolved. It becomes clear that the riddle has its origin in the twindom of the Melsztyński brothers, both of whom bear the same first name and neither of whom knows about the other's existence at the moment when the link between the lives of both Ludomir Melsztyńskis is exposed. At that point the protagonists' actions, experiences and utterances are once again, as in the Krzewin section of the plot, dominated by unity and unambiguity. Prior to this, they continue to be strongly self-contradictory.

It is interesting that the solving of the riddle concerning the obscured identity of Ludomir lends the interplay of unity and unambiguity with duality and ambiguity, a form of twinned tension. This is because the twindom of the Melsztyński brothers, i.e. the essence of the riddle finally revealed, provides at the same time the basic model for the mutual infiltration between unity and duality within the protagonists' paired relationships which underlie the riddle. There is an underlying symmetry in the fact that the solution to the riddle lies in the twindom of the Melsztyński brothers, whereas its subject matter is both Ludomir's obscured identity and Malvina and Ludomir's wavering reciprocity. After all, reciprocated affection implies a relationship between two people whose core is "twinned" unity in duality and, simultaneously, the same kind of duality in unity. Malvina and Ludomir's reciprocal affection is fulfilled in the undisturbed, perfect interlocking of their personal independence and co-dependence. It is only Ludomir's invasion of the perfect harmony of this equilibrium that terminates it. A consequence of this situation is, initially, the personal unity of Malvina and Ludomir represented by Krzewin, followed by the internal split in Malvina as a person that happens in Warsaw, which parallels the split in Ludomir as a person.

The very same symmetry underlies the riddle and the phenomena which its solution reveals. It appears that everything that disturbed the "twinned" unity in the relationship between Malvina and Ludomir was actually a reversal of the ideal "twinned" unity which had joined the parents of the Melsztyński brothers in the previous generation. The novel's close is preceded not only by the solution to the riddle, but also by a resumption of harmony in Malvina and Ludomir's relationship (which parallels that between the parents of the Melsztyński brothers). In the novel's final section, two marriages: of Malvina to Ludomir and of Wanda to not-Ludomir, are the beginning of two new incarnations of the "twinned" co-existence between personal unity and duality, but in the next generation.

One cannot resist the impression that Wirtemberska took twindom as her fundamental ludic and cognitive perspective. I have demonstrated that, while twindom constitutes the prime mover of the riddle, it is also the originator of the conflicts in the world in which the riddle reveals itself as a riddle. In this connection between the cognitive and ludic planes, with reference to twindom, an important cultural pattern should be noted. And we also see important evidence of Wirtemberska's own views on how novels affect their readers. Wirtemberska believed that ludic components created an appropriate mood in a novel for the final point to be able to be accepted by readers: "prescriptions, truths, lessons, which may be found in a romance under the mantle of entertainment" (3). This takes me back to an issue previously outlined in this study.

The ancient origin of the symbolism of twins is well known. This symbolism draws on types and fundamental components of imagery that have come down to us from the mythologies of primal peoples. These include twins known from folklore, such as the Slavic Lel and Polel; from ancient writings, such as Romulus and Remus; or from Biblical texts, such as Cain and Abel. The ancient world abounded in divine twins, while human twins feature heavily in the ancient and modern Christian world. In the ancient world, the symbolic function of twins as independent yet utterly similar beings focused on the "unification of opposites". As Vyacheslav Ivanov has pointed out, in ancient and archaic myths, twins symbolise "transitional links" between such primary cultural opposites as, for instance, odd and even, left and right, masculine and feminine (1978; 1987, 174–176; cf. Tokarev 358–359). In discussing both types of myth concerned directly with divine twins, Ivanov stresses that these creatures frequently became founders of whole families; in their actions and activities, "they often duplicated one another"; they embodied the interlocking of two family genealogies, "two beginnings" (1987, 174). Another issue raised by Ivanov is that in several archaic and ancient myths, dual supernatural creatures played simultaneously the part of twins and of Androgynes. In other words, they were cast in the role of two creatures representing one, and in the role of one creature representing two (1987, 174).

Twin-related motifs abound in literary texts from Antiquity until the present day. Yet the sources of their meaningful content tend to vary in different texts. They may relate to the already mentioned mythical, archaic and ancient symbolisms, folklore or Christian symbolism. Likewise, typical ways of using these motifs in literature tend to vary. There is no single tradition. Ivanov's ideas are again germane on this point. He claims that, in literature, in twin-related motifs, the archaic, dual symbolism merges with the problem of "a human doppelgänger (a human shadow)" (Ivanov 1987, 174). This seems to be confirmed both by the complex way in which Wirtemberska uses the twin brother motif and by the cultural context of the transitional period in which she realized her project.

Wirtemberska's ludic use of the twin brother motif, in order to produce a mysterious plot, one which abounds in misconstrued actions by the protagonists and situational complications, is typical. It resonates with solutions used over the centuries (for example, in Plautus' *The Brothers Menaechmus* and Shakespeare's *Comedy of Errors*). The additional, cognitive use which she makes of twindom as a central motif, casting it in the role of antecedent to her novel's conflicts, also situates itself within the time-honoured convention. This may explain why it was so accurately represented and interpreted by the novel's illustrator.

The essence of plot-related complications in *Malvina*, as I have shown, is the interweaving of parallels between the protagonists. On the one hand, this affects, explicitly, both siblings (Malvina and Wanda) and the two individuals in love (Malvina and Ludomir). On the other hand, less explicitly, it is about the relationships between parents and children, that is the grandparents and parents of the Ludomir brothers, and between the twins themselves. These numerous interconnections between the characters form the foundation for the "twinned" intermingling of the parallel and non-parallel personality traits, actions, and sometimes even utterances of the protagonists. This is one of the factors creating the impression of the multiple game of unity and unambiguity with duality and ambiguity, which I have already outlined. In the Malvina-Ludomir couple, the "twinned" parallel between personality traits, actions, and – in their case particularly – utterances, is broken. I have referred several times to the consequences of this shift. As we remember, the opposition of Ludomir and Ludomir, and consequently – of Malvina and Malvina, gives an explicit doppelgänger touch to the couple's past relationship. Malvina with respect to Ludomir, and Ludomir with respect to Malvina, both play their simultaneous parts on two opposing planes: the Warsaw plane and the Krzewin plane. To each other, they become split persons: at those moments when the Warsaw Ludomir comes across as the Krzewin Ludomir, Malvina finds him puzzling and inaccessible; when Malvina meets the Warsaw Ludomir, she in turn becomes puzzling and inaccessible to him. The split in the person of Ludomir within the "twin" Malvina-Ludomir couple is one of the explicit components of the plot, while the split in the person of Malvina is one of the less explicit.

The episode which recapitulates all the previous manifestations of this doppelgänger game, and simultaneously highlights the circumstances which explain its origin, is the finale of the Warsaw plot. As in the entire novel, so too in this episode, the events and Malvina's resulting experiences are recounted both in the narrator's tale and in the heroine's letter. Malvina's private conversation with one Ludomir is disrupted by a scream from the other Ludomir, an alter ego of the former. The scream becomes an integral component of the utterance which Malvina formulates, marked by a genuine turn to the Ludomir with whom she was actually conversing. Her utterance was to have communicated her emotional commitment, but is instead disrupted and followed by the heroine's loss of consciousness:

Rais[ing] her eyes, [she gave] the Prince her hand and declare[d]:
"Return safely, Prince, and when the war is over..."
But her words were cut short by an horrendous shriek as the most extraordinary apparition confounded her senses. In the dense thicket of the hedge, clearly illuminated by the moonlight, Malvina saw standing opposite her a second image of Ludomir. (132)

The letter in which the heroine quotes the unuttered part of her promise demonstrates that her simultaneous hearing and seeing of the two Ludomirs was, to her, equivalent to facing that which divided and split herself – having divided and split the person of the Ludomir she had encountered in Warsaw:

> I meant to add, "...and when the war is over, you will receive my hand." But I was unable to conclude these final words. My words were interrupted, interrupted perhaps forever, by an appalling scream and by a supernatural apparition, whose appearance dumbfounded my senses at the time, and whose memory has thrown me into a terrified panic ever since. I suddenly saw Ludomir's image reproduced behind him; despair and death were written on his face; he was lit up by the moonlight and seemed to emerge out of the darkness of the night. (136–137)

Malvina's letter allows me to conclude that this very incident forced her to face the duality of the Warsaw Ludomir as a problem of one and the same person, and of two different persons at the same time. Malvina depicts the other Ludomir as "a supernatural apparition" (136), and yet – as in the split second when she sees him, she denies the reality of that impression by refusing to accept the sighting of the other Ludomir as "hallucination", and not "all too real" (138). In the process, she resorts to self-accusation: the more she accepts the thought of the other Ludomir's real existence, the more she blames herself for having made a promise to the first:

> Agh, Wanda, that loathsome ghost returned to me along with my memory and has made such a deep impression on my mind that, even if I were to lose my memory, I would never shake it off. Wanda! Believe me, it was no hallucination. Wanda, it could have been an unhappy omen for Ludomir... an omen perhaps for Malvina, as well as an early punishment for the fact that her lips were about to utter something other than what her soul felt, and that she was about to give her hand to Prince Melsztyński when she was no longer able to give him her heart! (137)

The setting of the incident recalled by the heroine resembles the circumstances in which the mythological offspring of the Moon, the four-armed and four-legged Androgynes, who combined masculine with feminine traits, were cut in two by Zeus, assisted by Apollo. This mythological incident is thus narrated by Aristophanes in Plato's *Symposium*:

> [Zeus] proceeded to cut everyone in two, just as people cut up sorb-apples for preserving or slice eggs with a hair. As he divided them he told Apollo

to take each separated half and turn round the face and half neck to the cut side, so that each person by contemplating its own cut surface might behave more moderately. (2008, 23)

Roland Barthes elucidates that it was Zeus' intention to force the divided, two-armed and two-legged Androgynes to be continually reminded of their inner division. In Zeus' order, Barthes sees the prototypical inner imperative which insists that humans try to mentally control all that divides and splits them: *"Understand your madness*: that was Zeus' command when he ordered Apollo to turn the faces of the divided Androgynes (like an egg, a berry) toward the place where they had been cut apart (the belly)" (2001, 60; italics original). I point here to the mythical and problematic context of the incident recalled by the heroine, because components analogous to the mythological ones may be found in *Malvina*. Moreover, a violent change should be noted in Malvina's attitude towards the object of her affections: a riddle involving not one but two different individuals. It shows that she understands where she might have erred: she was guilty not of misconstruing the doppelgänger inconstancy of the Ludomir whom she encountered in Warsaw, but of misconstruing his identity.

This is how the final scene of the Warsaw plot endorses Ivanov's argument concerning the merging of archaic twin symbolism with the motif of the human doppelgänger in contemporary literature. The scene also endorses his belief that one component of this both ancient and modern problem is the inner co-existence of the duality of twins (two persons to represent one) and the androgynous duality (one person to represent two).

At this point let me draw attention to one more problematic complication of the motif of twins in Wirtemberska's novel. Interesting and important as it is, its content is associated with the twin motif popular during Classicism, which developed subsequently during the Enlightenment. In Wiremberska's novel, as in Molière's comedy *Amphitryon,* this complication depends on the connection between twins and doppelgängers, i.e. on a game of personal unity and duality, as well as symptoms of crisis in the institution of marriage. Jacques Lacan was the first to note and discuss these issues in relation to Molière's play (Lacan 1991). In Lacan's view, in the eighteenth century, the essence of the parallel between twindom and marriage lay in the latter's failure to engage with the ethical categories of "love", "constancy", or "commitment". In other words, in society's view, this bred the clash between strict moral requirements related to marriage and the more relaxed requirements related to concubinage. In *Malvina*, problems related to marriage are presented, as in *Amphitryon*, in the same context of the twin and doppelgänger interplay of personal unity and duality, which demonstrates that we are indeed dealing here with a range of issues and symbols that loomed large to people of the seventeenth and eighteenth centuries. Lacan claims that, following Molière's *Amphitryon*, an adaptation of Plautus, European thought became permeated with the idea of viewing marriage in two contradictory ways. One was to see it as a "verbal pact", solemnised during the wedding ceremony; the other – as the cause of most human conflicts. Lacan believes that this way of viewing marriage was encouraged by the mythological plot of Molière's *Amphitryon*, which revolves around the doppelgänger rivalry between gods and humans, just as in the play by Plautus and the ancient myth of Amphitryon.

Jupiter incarnated as Amphitryon, Alcmene's husband, fulfils the latter's marital obligations. Mercury, Jupiter's supporter, in turn, becomes a doppelgänger of Sosie, Amphitryon's servant and the husband of Cleanthis, Alcmene's servant. Unexpectedly, the basis of the marriages between Alcmene and Amphitryon, as well as between Cleanthis and Sosie, becomes, Lacan tells us, the "mirroring" of constancy and inconstancy. Out of dual love for Amphitryon, Alcmene bears "a double fruit" (1991, 270), i.e. twins. Lacan believes that the whirlpool of doppelgängers, which in Molière's play sucks the married couples in, is a model for the doppelgänger interplay of desires and fulfilments. In real life, this is an inseparable part of the spouses' subconscious, and consequently it exposes them to conflicts with the essence of the marriages in which they continue to live. In defining the essence of marriage as a "symbolic pact" (1991, 261), with all its implications, Lacan claims:

> But there is a conflict between this symbolic pact and the imaginary relations which proliferate spontaneously [...] This conflict subtends, one might say, the great majority of the conflicts in that milieu within which the vicissitude of the bourgeois destiny is unravelled, since it occurs within the humanist perspective of the realisation of the ego, and as a consequence within the alienation proper to the ego. (1991, 261)

In Lacan's view, Molière's Amphitryon plot – through a reversal of the role of Jupiter, "the sovereign of the Gods", who competes with earthly married couples – paradoxically highlights the role of the deity as sanctifier of marriage. Lacan says: "For the couple to keep to the human level, there has to be a god there" (1991, 263). The final speech of Molière's Jupiter, made in the presence of Sosie, addressed to Amphitryon, full of deceit and ambiguity, but also highlighting events of the past, corroborates Lacan's opinion. Let me quote a passage from that speech as Wirtemberska must have been familiar with both the original version of Molière's comedy and its superb Polish translation by Franciszek Zabłocki (1783):

> A share with Jupiter has nothing that in the least dishonours, for doubtless, it can be but glorious to find one's self the rival of the sovereign of the Gods. I do not see any reason why your love should murmur; it is I, God as I am, who ought to be jealous in this affair. Alcmene is wholly yours, whatever means one may employ; it must be gratifying to your passion to see that there is no other way of pleasing her than to appear as her husband. Even Jupiter, clothed in his immortal glory, could not by himself undermine her fidelity; what he has received from her was granted by her ardent heart only to you (Molière 1904).

In Wirtemberska's novel, the entire complex cognitive process, in which Malvina becomes involved as a result of the doppelgänger inconstancy of Ludomir's character, takes place between her first and second marriages – between an unhappy and a happy one. Malvina is a widow when she first meets Ludomir and when she finally marries him after many tribulations. I have intentionally played down these opening and concluding elements of the plot because I believe that only now can their proper significance be grasped – once we know how far the essence of the novel's mysterious plot complications oscillates between idealisation and trivialisation of the emotional bond between the protagonists. What depends on their lively mutual acceptance in this dual relationship, appears to be a certain compensation for the failure of the heroine's first marriage. What in their relationship depends on the salon lovers' game, conversely, warns of another potential similar failure. The heroine's first marriage, arranged by her parents, was a complete failure of the ideal of reciprocal marital love when confronted by reality. This consisted in, as the narrator puts it, "inept attempts at love" (19), and this flawed relationship was accepted by both parties. Hence the heroine's achievement of happiness in her second marriage, of which the narrator informs the reader at the novel's close, is a victory for the ideal dear to the heroine, for a love which continues to be alive and fulfilled. The salon type of love, strikingly common, and the emotional void of Malvina's first marriage, hidden from the world, are the losers:

Neither time nor the years, however, altered that powerful, exclusive love for Ludomir, which had so taken root in Malvina's heart since the day she first set eyes on him; she was likewise loved by him to the end of her days with that all-embracing love whose magic fills our lives, the world, every day, every hour with bewitching happiness, but which usually never lasts too long... (201)

The narrator states quite clearly that the relationship between Malvina and Ludomir relies on the perfect complementation of their affections, without any reservations. One cannot help thinking that, as the narrator closes her description of this love in two perfectly balanced clauses, she means to say that the protagonists have created for themselves a state of constant emotional fulfilment, which – in her view – tends not to last in marriage. One cannot help thinking too that the narrator wishes to declare that it is in this very fulfilment that the personal unity of the married protagonists reveals itself. (Let us note in passing that the Polish language has a name for this kind of psychological situation: *jednia małżeńska* [conjugal unity]). After all, the perfect complementation of both protagonists brings to mind the image of the Androgynes before they were cut in two by Zeus, as well as the image of the uncut fruit, to which they are compared in Plato. It is striking that the narrator ends her tale of the protagonists' conjugal happiness with an account of an incident, which – even if momentarily, yet unequivocally – disturbs the harmony between them. Here I mean Ludomir's silent complaint against Malvina, grounded in her alleged interest in Ludomir's doppelgänger, Prince Melsztyński (201). Both the space allocated to the episode in the narrator's tale and the fact that it centres around the word "ungrateful", which as we remember carries dual and heavily loaded emotional meaning for both protagonists, reveal that the issues commented on in Lacan's discussion of Moliere's comedy are also pertinent here:

Engrossed in these pranks and amused by his frivolity, Malvina seemed to Ludomir more absorbed with Prince Melsztyński than usual, and this affected him acutely. Malvina did not pay any attention to this immediately; but when she glanced at her husband she saw an expression of sadness on his face. It was the first moment since their marriage that she had noticed such an expression on his face; this dismayed her all the more. Malvina's heart at once understood Ludomir's heart; sincerely moved, she seized his hand:

"Ungrateful!" she said quietly with tears in her eyes.

That word, which had already passed sentence on his life twice before, now for the third time – and forever after – was to have the power to reassure his heart completely, filling it with the truest happiness which nothing further could extinguish. (201)

One more detail related to the Warsaw part of the plot of *Malvina* should be stressed here in order to supplement my discussion of its milestones. The beginning and middle points of the Warsaw plot are those moments in which a major role is played by Malvina's response to the qualities of Ludomir's speech (at the beginning) and then by the mutual responses of them both to the written qualities of the shared aphorisms (in the middle). In the final section of the Warsaw plot, discussed above, the centre of attention is again Malvina's response to audible utterances by the two Ludomirs, a fragment of the marriage proposal and the scream.

Let us note that the scream contains no hint, unlike the marriage proposal, that it is meant for Malvina; it could as well be aimed at any possible audience, including the screamer. Yet Malvina's response to it is much stronger than her response to the utterance which carries a clear confession, which shows that she recognises the screamer and the appeal made to her in the scream, despite the incident's "supernatural" quality. Let us also note that Malvina, when inclined to believe that there are two Ludomirs, is driven by impressions similar to those by which she was driven when assessing two doppelgänger incarnations of one Ludomir. This time, however, she appears more sensitive to the mental experience manifested in the intense directness of the spoken-aloud aspect of verbal utterance, the facial expression, gestures and body language, than to merely verbal content. This is why the Ludomir who screams, and not the one who proposes to her, comes across to her as a sentient being, experiencing genuine emotional agitation.

The most interesting aspect of the structure of *Malvina's* Warsaw plot is precisely the fact that, at all its milestones, a major role is played by the qualities of the utterances or messages formulated by the protagonists. The course of events unfolds in such a way that despite the appearance of the protagonists' mutual understanding, their verbal communications are a constant source of emotional, moral and aesthetic conflict. That is why at the various milestones in the Warsaw plot, their attention turns directly to the very qualities of utterances and messages, whether spoken or written, verbal or non-verbal.

The final scene of the Warsaw plot only confirms this structural principle. Let us note that the extraordinary quality of Malvina's experience results not only from her encounter with the apparition, but also from her encounter with the message which the apparition expresses through the scream, and she – by falling silent, all within the marriage proposal scene. We now know that the apparition scene anticipates the complete solution to the riddle, and consequently the resolution of the novel's plot. From this point of view, another structural characteristic should be noted: in this scene, Malvina – before anyone else around her, and based only on her own conflicting impressions – discovers that there are two Ludomirs. Other characters learn this only after the witnesses to the Melsztyński brothers' birth come forward, and after the visible proof of their personal separateness the birthmark which one of the brothers has and the other does not is produced.

When Wirtemberska presents the scream and the following silence in the final episode of the Warsaw plot – as when she presents the exchange of aphorisms and small talk in the preceding episodes – she stays within the range of problems raised by pre-romantic theoreticians of language, particularly Jean Jacques Rousseau and Johann Gottfried von Herder.

To Rousseau, the scream was an absolutely primeval mode of linguistic communication. Maria Renata Mayenowa, when discussing this opinion of his, writes:

> The emotion drew a scream from the breast of primeval man. Moreover, this emotional characteristic of language helps explain that the sound is its actual matter. A human being can influence other human beings through movement and through the voice. The movement is the touch and the gesture. But the touch is limited by the length of the arm. This leaves us with the gesture and the voice as the natural material of human expression, or more strictly speaking, with visual and acoustic signs. (1970, 18; trans. M.O.)

Jacques Derrida, when referring to the same idea of Rousseau, takes a similar stand. He claims that, in human interaction through language, Rousseau saw first and foremost the complementarity of gesture and word: "the visible gesture, more natural and more expressive, can join itself as a supplement to speech, which is itself a substitute for gesture" (1997, 235). It combines, in Derrida's view, the process of perfecting the language with the reinforcement of the communicative complementarity of gesture and word: "it separates gesture and speech primitively united in the mythic purity, absolutely immediate and therefore natural, of the cry" (Derrida 1997, 235). Rousseau was therefore convinced, I claim following Derrida and Mayenowa, that in the endless multiplicity of communicative situations made possible by the use of language, the exchange between components which are more and less natural, or more and less expressive, is of utmost significance. These components can come from both sides: according to Derrida, both through the gesture and through the word, and according to Mayenowa – both through visual signs (gestures) and acoustic signs (the voice). Derrida, when enlarging on Rousseau's view on "*substituting* for [gestures] the articulate sounds of the voice" (1997, 235; italics original), writes: "Everything in language is substitute, and this concept of substitute precedes the opposition of nature and culture: the supplement can equally well be natural (gesture) as artificial (speech)" (1997, 235). It can thus be said, following these interpretative suggestions, that for Rousseau human communication, when separated from its mythical origins, arises every time from natural resources of expression, which used to be the loci of mythical behaviour. It arises even when it is not a scream or the falling of silence. According to Rousseau, this occurs in every situation in which humans communicate through language. In contrast, the kind of wholly individuated language communication which Wirtemberska presents, i.e. the scream and the following silence, is for Rousseau a more or less conscious re-enactment of the mythical behaviours. This is because it carries the marks of source expression, resting on the borderline between internal and external agitation, memory and imagination, appearances and reality. Derrida, commenting on Rousseau's pronouncement that a gesture, unlike the voice, is characterised by "less depend[ence] on conventions" (1997, 235), writes: "The gesture, that of passion rather than that of need, considered in its purity of origin, guards us against an already alienating speech, a speech already carrying in itself death and absence" (1997, 234).

Herder, in his polemic with Rousseau, opposes locating the sources of linguistic expression in the scream ("Treatise on the Origin of Language"). He locates them, on the contrary, in human reason and its most important quality, sense. Referring to the *ratio* and *oratio formulas,* he writes: "If no reason was possible for the human being without language, good!, then the invention of the latter is as natural, as old, as original, as characteristic for the human being as the use of the former" (Herder 2004, 91). At the same time, Herder links the very existence of language, its historical origin as well as the entire sphere of living language communication with the influence of human sensual sensibility. He argues:

In more than one language *word* and *reason, concept* and *word, language* and *originating cause* [*Ursache*], consequently also share one name, and this synonymy contains its whole genetic origin. With the Easterners it became the most everyday idiom to call the *acknowledgment* of a thing *name-giving*, for in the bottom of the soul both actions are one. They call the human being the *speaking* animal, and the nonrational animals the *dumb*. [...] In this way language becomes a *natural organ of the understanding*, a *sense of the human soul*. (2004, 96–97; italics original)

Herder concludes: "We are a single thinking *sensorium commune*, only touched from various sides" (2004, 106; italics original). It must be stated that the main assumption behind this argument is the belief that "feeling forms the basis of all the senses" (2004, 106). The coexistence of human reflection, thinking and sensuality, affections and fancy is thus depicted by Herder:

> The normal course of our thoughts proceeds so quickly, the waves of our sensations rush so obscurely into each other, there is so much in our soul at once, that in regard to most ideas we are as though asleep by a spring where to be sure we still hear the rush of each wave, but so obscurely that in the end sleep takes away from us all noticeable feeling. If it were possible for us to arrest the chain of our thoughts and look at each link for its connection, what strange phenomena!, what foreign analogies among the most different senses – in accordance with which, however, the soul habitually acts! (2004, 106)

For Herder, as for Rousseau, language is an outlet for the natural human need for expression, particularly emotional, and communication. According to Rousseau, in order to satisfy this need, constant cooperation between the changeable expressive values of language and non-linguistic means of communication, such as intonation, the meaning of gestures, the symbolism of any involved objects, as well as the time and place in which the communication takes place, is required. Rousseau views the expressive diversity of means of communication in connection, on the one hand, with the natural diversity of the human senses to which they speak selectively; on the other – with the wealth and complexity of human communicative behaviour. According to Herder, however, natural expression through language corresponds primarily to the diversity of human experience, feeling and thought. Herder also believes that neither the operation of individual senses nor the expressive qualities of means of communication, formed in conjunction with them, can be separated. Hence when Rousseau stresses the external conditioning of language communication, Herder emphasises its internal conditioning.

In the interlocking of diverse inner experiences, feelings and thoughts, Herder sees them as agents of communication. Herder scholars remain in agreement on these issues. Jan Sikora explains that by the "unity of language and thought Herder means the unity of a person's language and whole psyche, manifest in literary and scholarly work, and primarily in the particular speech process" (1970, 69; trans. M.O.). Zofia Florczak maintains that to Herder language is the expression of the human soul, "which first experiences an action and only then the acting agent" (1978, 64; trans. M.O.). Notwithstanding these differences, Rousseau and Herder share the view that language was not born only out of practical need and does not exclusively serve the purpose of reasoning. Both set out to describe phenomena which testify to the fact that language use, particularly if individuated in some way, expresses intentions, desires, feelings – in a word, affections. It is significant that both Rousseau and Herder see language as "created for the heart rather than for reason", with a greater capacity to charm than to rationally explain, participating just as easily in the supernatural as in the more commonplace, as well as closely connected to both mythical (Rousseau) and metaphysical (Herder) behaviours.

In Wirtemberska's novel, the apparition episode is constructed in such a way that it maintains a close connection between the supernatural quality of the events and the temporary states of the protagonists' speech as they participate in those events. The scream of the ghostly Ludomir and the falling silent of Malvina, preceded by the interruption to her utterance addressed to the real Ludomir, deprive the situation of any normally expected sense. The scream and the falling silent play the role of messages which destroy a sense of reality, yet remain at the same time truly personal. They constitute a transitional phase between the movements of the protagonists' faces and bodies and their verbal utterances. In this way, the original and hence very personal nature of both types of communication is expressed. And it is achieved through the references of both protagonists to the mythical and metaphysical aspects of speech, as conceived by Rousseau and Herder.

Part Three
Malvina, or the Heart's Intuition

> And if the author after a tangled plot
> Lets the loving pair join at last together
> – Adam Mickiewicz, "To M***"

The Ubiquitous Twinning

The ultimate explanation of the twinning of *Malvina's* protagonists restores the disrupted continuity of their individual fates. It clearly puts an end to what constitutes the source of the narrative's splitting into the narrator's tale and the protagonists' letters: the double identity of the male protagonist, the coherence and incoherence of certain events – in a word, the mystifying break-up and complication of events. It is not so easy to notice, however, that along with the final explanation of the protagonists' twinning – the interlocking of the author's and the narrator's representational and interpretative acts, in consequence of which the reader learns about the course of the events, likewise comes to an end.

I shall now focus on the ubiquity of the twinned interlocking of personal unity and duality in *Malvina*. It influences the connections between the protagonists as well as those between the author and the narrator, which are in both cases twinned – literally and metaphorically. I shall also focus on the correspondences between the interlocking of personal unity and duality on *Malvina's* two "planes", i.e. in the events and in the narrative which presents and interprets these events in the novel's overall composition.

This does not change the fact that what I have just outlined forms the very essence of *Malvina's* plot complications. The focus of these complications surrounding the twin couple of male protagonists and the "twinned" interlocking of personal correspondences and opposites within the familial, emotional and social connections between the characters, has been given careful attention in the previous part of this book. Let me now recapitulate the essence of these complications. The incarnation of one Ludomir Melsztyński into two completely different persons, which confuses Malvina, is closely connected with her unshakeable faith in the reciprocity of feelings which is, to her, a symbol of personal unity between two individuals. These two phenomena, in turn, are closely connected with the theatricality of the salon milieu, whose aim is to play with the personal unity of its participants, of both primary and secondary characters.

This "twinned" interlocking of personal unity and duality in the narrative and composition of *Malvina* is demonstrated by the role played on this formal plane of the novel by the dual identity of Maria Wirtemberska herself, split into the authorial persona and the narrator. Let me stress once again that on the plane of events, a crucial role is played in the novel by the dual identity of the male protagonist, split into the twins of Ludomir Prince Melsztyński and Ludomir "Little Flame". Let me begin by describing the manifestations of this dual identity, in other words – the "twinned duality", of Maria Wiremberska.

Maria Wiremberska's creative act is the writing of her novel. The results of this act, i.e. the novel entitled *Malvina, or the Heart's Intuition*, are discussed in her preface, which takes the form of a letter addressed *To My Brother*. The narrator's creative act, in turn, is the telling of events related to complexities in the lives of three characters: Malvina and the Melsztyński twin brothers, drawing on their own letters and letters written by other characters. The narrator repeatedly informs the reader that when relating these events, she is performing in fact a novelistic act *par excellence*. She wishes to be recognised not only as the narrator of the events that she knows about, but also as the creator of the form in which they function in the novel: as somebody who consciously juxtaposes what she has to say about the events with what the participants in these events have said about the events in their own letters – a persona whose reflections, remarks and opinions derive from the reflections, remarks and opinions contained in these letters. The narrator's creative invention would seem to cover the majority of novelistic acts, from the shaping of multiple turns in the plot within both the tale and the letters, through collating passages from the letters as well as entire letters, to the arrangement of the novel's chapters.

Let me quote a few utterances by the novel's narrator, in which she reports on the forms assumed by the narrative selected and composed by herself. The first of these utterances, inserted between two letter fragments, shapes the arrangement of these letter fragments and of the novel's chapters; the second determines the turn of the narrative from the tale to the letter; the third determines the ordering of the chapters; while the fourth, occurring at the beginning of a chapter, influences the form of the tale contained within it. It is significant that in all these passages, as in other similar passages, the narrator refers to both the protagonists and the readers at the same time.

Here is the first example:

"But enough of all that, which has grieved you much too much; far better to listen to my account of yesterday, opportune for myself, since on that day I was able to make myself useful."

Here Ludomir described what the Reader knows from the previous chapter about how he met Malvina for the first time. He went on:

"In the dazzling glare of the fire, amongst the smoke and collapsed beams..." (15)

The second example:

In order to better understand the curious and contradictory thoughts and emotions that Malvina was undergoing in such circumstances, I shall extract a portion of her letter to Wanda. Not wishing to overstretch the Reader's patience, I shall not transcribe the whole.

Extract from Malvina's letter to her Sister
"Oh, Wanda! How little real happiness is contained in this fashionable world which we imagined so prepossessing!" (64)

The third:

She anticipated Ludomir's warmth and gratitude with inexpressible happiness. Exhausted by the trials of the day she finally fell asleep, bathed in these happy thoughts. And since my Malvina is taking a rest, I too will pause for a while before I begin my next chapter. (90)

The fourth:

Chapter Twenty-Eight: "The End"
Maybe to some of my Readers Ludomir's conversation with Malvina appears
too long; but, alas, few such happy hours occur in life! Let us therefore not
begrudge our lovers the happy hour they spent so contentedly together; it
may have been too long for the Reader, but for them it flew past like lightning.
And as for myself, I shall make up for their fault by attempting to describe
as succinctly as I can the remaining twists that fate has since then wrought
upon the lives of Ludomir, Malvina, and all the other characters mentioned
in the course of my novel. (195)

In utterances such as the above, the narrator styles herself as the
novelist. The narrative and epistolary discourse is thereby situated within
Wirtemberska's original discourse. This shows, internally, what is hap-
pening within the primary source from which the novel with its heterogeneous narrative discourse originates. This is because Wirtemberska,
when writing her novel – that is, transforming written discourse into her
story-telling and epistolary discourse, styles herself as the narrator. It is
within these references, which demonstrate an active interdependence,
rather than a merely passive coexistence, of the discourses realised by
Wirtemberska and the narrator, that the essence of the novel's essential
"twindom" is to be found. Put in more literal terms, it could be said that
these two discourses appear homologous and analogous at the same
time. The connections formed between them, regardless of whether we
view them through the novel's metaphor of twindom, or through the
logical notions of homology and analogy, accentuate the perfect interlocking of these discourses, given their apparent sameness.[27] Even when

---

27 The notions of homology and analogy, taken from logic and used here to depict the interrela-
    tions between the authorial and narratorial discourses, are frequently called upon in language
    and culture studies. They are especially useful when it is necessary to determine particularly
    complex correspondences between certain phenomena. Here I mean correspondences which,
    while allowing for the occurrence of similarities and differences within features or manifesta-
    tions of particular phenomena, deny the sameness of these phenomena themselves. In structur-
    al studies of languages and cultures, considering the nature of such complex correspondences
    is essential. Hence the propositions put forward by Sergej Karcevskij, a pioneer of structural
    linguistics, seem viable: "Opposition pure and simple necessarily leads to chaos and cannot
    serve as the basis of a system. True differentiation presupposes a simultaneous resemblance
    and difference. Concepts form a series founded on a common element and are opposed only
    within this series" (1982, 51). Regardless of the distinctiveness of major twentieth-century
    structural studies in language and culture, the notions of analogy and homology are used
    consistently to discuss similarities, on the one hand, and on the other – equivalent properties

the narrator's discourse imitates the original written discourse, it merely reflects the original. At the same time, it upholds its status as secondary discourse, derivative of the original, thereby confirming with its narrative and epistolary structure the purely written form of the other. The original discourse, which determines the form of the narratorial discourse, is the material and semantic element that enables the creative roles of the narrator and the author to co-exist, along with the former's acts of representation and interpretation, and the latter's parallel acts. In addition, on the basis of this original discourse, this co-existence pertains, firstly, to the broadly conceived identity of the narrator (a woman, a Pole, a competent storyteller and a moralist) as the origin of her creative activity; and secondly, to the hidden figure of the author, Maria Wirtemberska, as the intellectual source of the novel.

The Contrast between and the Irregular Pattern of the Tale and the Letters

The most conspicuous and general manifestation of the above is the fundamental compositional property of *Malvina*, expressed through the irregular, abruptly changing pattern of "shifts" from one narrative form to the other, i.e. from the tale to the letters (or vice versa). For the sake of brevity, I will refer to this particular feature as the oscillating pattern of the tale and the letters. This is punctuated by discrepancies between the arrangement of the novel's chapters and the ordering of the contrastive juxtapositions of the two narrative forms. Only at the novel's beginning do the chapters come together with an alternating succession of tale episodes and letters. In later chapters, this kind of symmetry is no longer found. The subsequent chapters, in particular their beginnings and endings, apportion segments of irregularly mixed sections of the tale and the letters, thereby forming an irregular, abruptly changing pattern of shifts between the two narrative forms. Without the chapter frames, the contrastive juxtapositions of the tale and the letters would not have taken their characteristic form, although they would have had the potential to arrange and interpret their content according to the principle of oppo-

---

or manifestations of the phenomena at issue. In speaking of apparently analogous discourses, I follow Ferdinand de Saussure's terminology, as recalled by Roland Barthes. As to issues related to the unmotivated meaning of language signs, Barthes points out that in the special case of onomatopoeia we deal with a "partly unmotivated" meaning, which de Saussure called "a relative analogy" (Barthes 1964, 111).

sites. In this way, the production of the novel *Malvina*, by allowing both the chapters and the contrastive turns of the plot to be simultaneously realized, lays the material and semantic foundations for the irregular pattern of alternating tale and letters to emerge.

On closer scrutiny, the irregular, oscillating pattern of tale and letters appears to be clearly delineated by certain interpretative manoeuvres, focused on the events portrayed. These manoeuvres connect doubly with both the author and the narrator, thereby affecting the portrayed events from the novel's two interlocking subjective and semantic standpoints. On the one hand, they are contained within the division of the narrative and the events into chapters, which are numbered and titled. On the other hand, they manifest themselves through the contrastive juxtapositions of the tale and the letters. The two types of interpretative manoeuvres are dualistic in essence. Let us note that one of these types, expressed through the division into numbered and titled chapters, which on the face of it remains within the competence of the narrator (as her discourse suggests), interlocks with the external events which she presents and interprets, thereby showing their connection not with one but with two novel-creating entities: the author and the narrator. The other type, i.e. the contrastive juxtapositions of the tale and the letters (seemingly used by the narrator as her own tool for the interpretation of the tales which she tells), does not exist outside the framework of these chapters, which contain an external interpretation of events within the competence of the author.[28]

The "twindom" of the connections between the personally and functionally disparate creative acts of the author and narrator constitutes for these interpretative manoeuvres a necessary point of reference. It lies neither in any particular storytelling act on the part of the narrator, based on the letters of the participants in the events, nor in the author's nov-

---

28 One might ask why I call these manoeuvres "interpretative". This notion, after all, seems better suited to purely critical rather than novelistic purposes. This stretching of the term, however, appears pertinent here as it highlights the "twinned" acts of the author and of the narrator, which resemble the methods of interpreting literary texts used in literary criticism. They rely on explication of the meaning of a literary work or its elements, formulated in metalanguage, that is the language superimposed on the language of the interpreted literary text. In *Malvina*, like in other novels, the authorial and narratorial interpretative manoeuvres constitute elements of the events to which they pertain, which makes them elements of the novelistic representation of these events. While these authorial and narratorial interpretations may not have the same metalanguage status as critical-literary explications of the events, they are formulated in the "languages" of composition and narration, higher on the "meta" level than the language of the events to which they pertain.

el-writing act, which yields that narrative and epistolary discourse. The point of reference is the very "twinned" co-existence and simultaneous disjointedness of these two acts, whose syntax and semantics are reflected in the crisscrossing of the contrastive juxtapositions of the tale and the letters with the sequence of titled chapters.

This is why I assume that the main compositional principle which organises and interprets the events in *Malvina* is the oscillating, repeated and irregular crisscrossing of the opposing semantic values of the tale and the letters, rather than their contrast itself. It should be remembered, however, that this principle of irregular switching is used in place of the principle of contrast in Malvina. This is due to the "twinned" complementariness of the author's and the narrator's interpretative manoeuvres, related to the portrayed events and consequently becoming inseparable elements of the presentation of those events. The primary, privileged field where this co-existence occurs is the appropriate sequence of events, which enables them to become the venue for the riddle to be resolved as well as providing symbolic content for its "subject matter" and "explanation". Let me also recall that, in order to shape Malvina's compositional principle of the oscillating tale and letters, the disjointedness of the author's and the narrator's interpretative manoeuvres, expressed through the different ways in which they operate, is as important as their interlocking as they complement each other. Although it is impossible to specify precisely where in the novel the influence of the former ends and that of the latter begins, their symptoms can however be identified.

The author's interpretative manoeuvres manifest themselves through the written quality of the novelistic discourse. The narrator's, in turn, emerge from the spoken and written properties of the discourse delivered by the narrator and the reflections, opinions and remarks which she verbalises *expressis verbis*. The author's interpretative manoeuvres are more scattered than the narrator's which is the result of their spatial distribution, beginning with the novel's title, preface and motto, down to the division of the narrative and event-related material into titled chapters. Both types of manoeuvre focus on verbal and non-verbal constituent parts. The author's manoeuvres centre around the constituent parts of the entire novel, separated according to events and spatial locations, such as the title, the preface, the motto, and above all – the chapters. The narrator's manoeuvres centre around the utterance-based and spatial turns between the spoken and written narrative forms. Undoubtedly, where the poetics informing these narrative turns meets the poetics informing the novel's chapters, there occurs a rather intangible interlocking of the author's and the narrator's interpretative manoeuvres.

The author's interpretative manoeuvres, encoded in the novel's title, preface and motto, serve to generalise the meanings behind the presented events prior to the spoken and written narrative discourse, which features purely utterance-based acts of event interpretation presented as reflections, remarks and opinions. A similar role to these previously striking generalisations with regard to successive stages of events, is played by the chapter headings. At this point, a comparison of the meaning and symbolism of the separate interpretative manoeuvres must be made. The essence of the author's manoeuvres is her impatient and demonstrative drawing of conclusions by means of the chapter-heading formulas, the preface and the motto, the participation of the protagonists in the mystifying events, equivalent to the calling into being of the novel as a whole. The essence of the narrator's interpretative manoeuvres lies, in contrast, in her patient and detailed commentary, which springs from meticulous observation of the participants in the mystifying events, corroborated by what they write in their letters.

This is how, schematically, the irregular pattern of shifts between the tale and the letters is delineated – by the essentially twinned influences of the author's and the narrator's interpretative manoeuvres, focused on the one hand on the division into chapters, and on the contrastive twists of the narrative, on the other. It must be added that in this schematic overview, the role of the chapter boundaries necessarily obscures the role of their titles. Similarly, the role which falls to the novel's narrative shifts – from tale to letters (or vice versa) – obscures the role of the reflections, opinions and remarks contained *expressis verbis* in these two kinds of narrative utterance.[29]

At the start of the novel, in the initial Krzewin-based section of the plot, the boundaries of the chapters alternate and coincide with some sections of the narrator's tale and with some sections of the protagonists' letters. This is why the pattern delineated by the shifts between these two narrative forms appears initially regular. Indirectly, this is also shown in the chapter headings, which in an alternating manner, either do or do not include the word "letter". Although the connections between the

---

29 Up to a point, these irregularities may be eliminated by insertion of a contents page, which would list the chapters and their titles. This may be helpful in following my discussion of the irregular oscillating pattern of the tale and letters. The 1822 edition of *Malvina* has no contents page, unlike twentieth-century editions of the novel (for instance, Witold Billip's 1978 edition and the 2012 English translation, which used Billip's edition).

overt and the implied aspects of the plot emerge in these early stages, this does not yet cause any event-related tension (Chapters One to Eight). The earliest sign of tension is the shift from the tale to the letter and back within one chapter (Chapter Nine). Similar shifts occur regularly as the narrative speed accelerates, and more and more metamorphoses of the male protagonist appear as plot complicating factors (Chapters Ten to Twenty-Two, especially Chapters Twelve, Thirteen and Seventeen). After that, the pattern delineated by the shifts between successive sections of the tale and successive letter fragments is subject to irregular break-ups and fragmentation. The chapters making up Volume One, which cover the rapid Warsaw-based section of the plot, feature respectively the tale; a juxtaposition of three letters; the tale complemented by a letter; the tale and a letter; and finally, the tale (Chapters Ten to Fourteen). The chapters of Volume Two pertaining to the same plot section contain, respectively, the tale complemented by a distinct spoken account and a letter; the tale and a letter; a letter complemented by the tale; the tale and a letter; a letter complemented by the tale; the tale; the tale once again; the tale again; a letter within the tale frame; and finally – the tale. Significantly, the titles of these chapters – unlike in the initial stage of the plot – do not reflect these continuing yet irregular shifts between the two narrative forms. The title of a chapter which contains three letters, does not contain the word "letter" at all (Chapter Eleven). In this group of chapters, the word "letter" occurs only once. Significantly, the chapter title which does contain it refers to an extraordinary letter: one which at the same time carries information and functions as an accessory to the plot in progress. In both these capacities, this letter contributes to the explanation of the male protagonist's inexplicable metamorphoses and resulting complexities (Chapter Eighteen). In the closing plot section, which allows the reader to understand the essence of these complexities, the chapters contain – apart from the narrator's tale and the protagonists' letters – a combination of separate spoken accounts and letters by secondary characters, who possess hitherto hidden knowledge about the male protagonist's childhood and parentage (Chapters Twenty-Two to Twenty-Eight). The first retrospective section of this type, which precedes the occurrence of events instrumental in the resolution of the plot complexities, is contained as early as Chapter Fifteen.

Where does this schematic outline lead us? It is not difficult to see that without the course of the shifting pattern delineated by the narrator's tale and the protagonists' letters there would be no plot fragmentation. Neither would there be any conflict between the explicit and hidden actions of the protagonists, or the repeated shifts experienced by the female protagonist during the plot's most rapid stage, between her perception of the appearances concerning the person of Ludomir and her intuition of the concealed reality. The pattern of irregular shifts between the tale and the letters ensures endurance of the riddle and its resolution at a later point: this is the compositional backbone of the riddle. It is no coincidence that it is adapted to suit the event-related lacunae which gradually become filled, and the intuition which defines the female protagonist's inner life.

It is more difficult to perceive that the irregular shifting between the tale and the letters functions as the novel's compositional backbone. Indeed, this conclusion ought to be as clear as the first: because the unquestionable relevance of the event-based riddle, as well as the cogent connections between the interpretative functions of the chapters, on the one hand, and the shifts between the narrative forms, on the other, are what actually make up the external and internal aspects of one novel, *Malvina*. The shifting pattern is determined both by the mystifying reality and by the consciousness of the eponymous heroine, who is trying to grasp it. But that is not all: the pattern is additionally determined by the novel's narrative forms, used to represent these aspects. The ultimate interdependence of these three aspects, impossible to render schematically, is revealed by the novel itself.

Sterne and Wirtemberska

The poetics of the novel's division into chapters and chapter structure are among the major themes of the digressions which abound in the tale told by the protagonist of Lawrence Sterne's *Life and Opinions of Mr. Tristram Shandy, Gentleman*. This superficially simple statement refers to a very complex issue, since the novel features an eccentric arrangement of chapters and a remarkable chapter structure. The digressions about the chapters, made by Sterne's protagonist who regards himself, in the act of writing his life and opinions, as the novel's protagonist, narrator and author, problematize major features of the text. On the face of it, *Tristram Shandy* appears to be made up of contradictory compositional elements. Each of the countless digressions draws the protagonist's autobiographical account into a course of events of its own, multiplying the number of temporal planes covered, the subjects discussed and the characters recalled in the novel. This multiplication of digressions interfering with the autobiographical account is governed by Tristram's train of thought. Let us remember that to him, his autobiography is a novelistic act, which is why he situates himself as its protagonist, narrator and author. In *The Rise of the Novel*, Ian Watt thus summarises the effects of Tristram's project: "the more he [Tristram] writes and the more we read, the more our common objective recedes" (1965, 292).

The Russian formalist Viktor Shklovsky believes that the key to understanding *Tristram Shandy*'s parody of contemporary novelistic techniques, is this very poetics of chapters, manifested both in the novel's form and the subject of the novel's digressions. Shklovsky sees it in the following way: as the division of the narrative and event-based material into chapters is a mere pretext for digressiveness on a variety of subjects, this explains why the chapters themselves are subject to ongoing digression. Let me now briefly explain the most striking eccentricities which bind together the two dimensions of the literary work: the form and the digression, according to Shklovsky (1991, 148–154).

In *Tristram Shandy*, some chapters are left out, abandoned or misplaced (this is also true of the preface and the dedication). Volume IV has no Chapter XXIV, and Chapter XXIII is followed directly by Chapter XXV. In that chapter, Tristram views these irregularities as positive:

> No doubt, Sir – there is a whole chapter wanting here – and a chasm of ten pages made in the book by it – but the book-binder is neither a fool, or a knave, or a puppy – nor is the book a jot more imperfect, (at least upon that score) – but, on the contrary, the book is more perfect and complete by wanting the chapter, than having it, as I shall demonstrate to your reverences in this manner. (2005, 282)

In the novel's final volume, Volume IX, Chapters XVIII and XIX do not follow Chapter XVII, but Chapter XXV instead. The length of the chapters varies greatly: some go on for several pages, while others contain only one or a couple of sentences at most. The chapters tend to be structurally complex, particularly when it comes to their beginnings and endings. For example, Chapter XXIII of Book I opens with this multi-layered statement from Tristram:

> I have a strong propensity in me to begin this chapter very nonsensically, and I will not balk my fancy. – Accordingly I set off thus.
> If the fixture of *Momus*'s glass, in the human breast... (2005, 64–65)

Shklovsky claims that *Tristram Shandy* offers a parodistic polemic against novelistic chapter arrangement according to the previously accepted, arbitrary principles of chronology, and not according to the rules developed by the author. Most fully, this contrast is presented in the "chapter upon chapters", that is Chapter X of Volume IV (1991, 253). Shklovsky claims that *Tristram Shandy* also fights against the novelistic course of events, ordered according to the very same principle of chronology which informs the arrangement of chapters. In *Tristram Shandy*, the digressions cause the events to run not along a straight line but a serpentine one. Another major target of the digressions, other than the poetics of chapters, is the perverse acceptance of the straight line as a model for courses of events which occur in real life and in literary works. This discussion in turn appears at its most comprehensive in Chapter XL of Volume VI (exclusively devoted to this issue).

Shklovsky recalls the following statement of Sterne, which explains how his text connects the opposing "worlds" of the story line and digression:

> By this contrivance the machinery of my work is of a species by itself; two contrary motions are introduced into it, and reconciled, which were thought to be at variance with each other. In a word, my work is digressive, and it is progressive too, – and at the same time. (1991, 63–64)

This is how, more recently, Paul Ricoeur views the transformation of the English novel in Sterne's day:

> well aware of what he was doing and a master of his art, [Richardson] could boast that there was no digression in his work that did not stem from its subject and also contribute to it, which is the formal definition of plot. (1985, 163)

Shklovsky believes that the key to understanding the compositional eccentricities of Sterne's second novel, *A Sentimental Journey through France and Italy*, lies in the titles and subtitles of the chapters (1964). In *Tristram Shandy*, the chapters are not titled – they are only numbered. *A Sentimental Journey* reverses this: its chapters are not numbered, but titled and subtitled in a repetitive manner. The recurrence of subtitles which contain only geographical names, such as Calais, Paris or Versailles, is less puzzling than the recurrence of chapter titles as such. It is easy to see that this prevents particular episodes in the journey from being translocated, which the protagonist relates beyond their correct spatial and temporal situation. The recurrence of chapter titles is of a different nature, and seems puzzling indeed, but is in fact deeply ustified.

Yorick the traveller, just like Tristram the descendant of the Shandy family, is the one-man protagonist, narrator and author of the literary text which he has undertaken to produce. He combines his travel account with a detailed, almost meticulous lecture on the impressions and opinions inspired by his experiences during the journey. The text contains chapters in which he recalls everything that has happened within and around him second by second, sensation by sensation. The recurrent titles, identical or similar, with which he labels the chapters of his travel account are footholds enabling him to muse longer on those observations and reflections which appeal to him the most out of the many. This is the case, for example, with the title sequence centred around the word "remise" in its obsolete sense of "coach house". Every time the reader of A Sentimental Journey encounters, at short intervals, titles such as "The Remise Door. Calais" (three times) or "The Remise. Calais" (three times), Yorick's account returns to the incident which has been occupying his mind for some time; if he did not give it sufficient attention, it would have been lost among the many more recent incidents, thereby failing to be understood by him. The incident at issue focuses on the tender sentiment, which at one particular moment binds Yorick to a female stranger, expressed through glances, conversation and the touching of hands. In one of the "remise" chapters, Yorick returns to this tender sentiment, which persists unaltered amid many other incidents, and informs the reader of some of its more minor elements:

> I fear, in this interval, I must have made some slight efforts towards a closer compression of her hand, from a subtle sensation I felt in the palm of my own – not as if she was going to withdraw hers – but, as if she thought about it – and I had infallibly lost it a second time, had not instinct more than reason directed me to the last resource in these dangers – to hold it loosely, and in a manner as if I was every moment going to release it, of myself. (2005, 604)

Hence *A Sentimental Journey*'s recurrent chapter titles, which head the chapters of Yorick's travel account, ought to be viewed as signposts which represent his trains of thought by isolating and facilitating his understanding of incidents, such as that moment of tender sentiment, whose actual duration must have been a matter of minutes. The recurring titles express the attitude of Yorick as author and as narrator towards his work in progress, in which he also features as a protagonist.

Sterne's two novels rely on the interplay between the cross-references to the interlocking acts of writing. When reading Sterne's *Tristram Shandy* and *Sentimental Journey*, we follow the novelistic acts of Tristram and Yorick, but this also works the other way around: when following the novelistic acts of Tristram and Yorick, we read Sterne's *Tristram Shandy* and *Sentimental Journey*. It is Sterne's interplay with these cross-references that underpins Shklovsky's analysis. Watt, who discusses only *Tristram Shandy*, likewise notes this phenomenon, although without giving it much space. He points to Sterne's "simple but ingenious expedient of locating his reflections in the mind of his hero" (1991, 293). Kazimierz Bartoszyński, a Polish Sterne scholar, while examining Yorick primarily as a narrator, by problematizing his creative acts, also documents their purely authorial and novelistic dimensions. He saturates his analysis, from which I quote below, with terminology meant to reflect the complexity of the narrator's "creative" acts:

> The "creative" process, which attracts so much attention, is viewed as a process of making choices out of many possibilities. Even when the narrator discusses his uncertainties, his "incapacity" and the spontaneity of his acts, when the fragmentariness of the presented reality comes to the fore and is accentuated *in medias res* by the chapter beginnings, all this is done with a view to stressing the creative nature of the text. (Bartoszyński 1977, 678; trans. M.O.)

In their more recent commentaries on Sterne, Paul Ricoeur and Marian Hobson attach considerable significance to the novelistic dualities of his writerly acts. They believe the dualities to have shaped contemporary views on novelistic illusion and disillusion, which I will discuss below (Ricoeur 1985; Hobson 1982).

My discussion of Sterne's art of novel writing is not coincidental here. Wirtemberska was not only a Sterne enthusiast, but also his conscious imitator. Jan Śniadecki, one of *Malvina*'s first reviewers, noted Wirtemberska's mastery of the intricate ways of plot development, first introduced by Sterne, in that she successfully combined several plot complexities. Importantly for us here, Śniadecki stressed the "peculiar" nature of chapter titles, modelled on Sterne's:

> The reader's attention and curiosity, forcefully grabbed at the beginning, grow gradually over the course of methodically unfolding events. Here, the

author was aided by imitating Sterne's method in his sentimental journey, where chapter titles strike the reader with their peculiarity but seem to have no connection with one another, and yet they manage to maintain a secret, happy knot as well as the order of things. (2003, 27; trans. M.O.)

Apart from Malvina, Wirtemberska's other text, *Niektóre zdarzenia, myśli i uczucia doznane za granicą* [Certain Events, Thoughts and Feelings Experienced Abroad], is entirely modelled on Sterne's *Sentimental Journey.* Both the composition and the plot, which make it a travel account, are directly linked to Sterne's book.[30] In *Malvina,* we also find direct references to Sterne's book. These occur at two points: in the structure of *Malvina*'s opening; and in the structure and content of Chapter Fourteen, entitled "Charity Collecting". The parallel between *Malvina*'s opening section (the female protagonist talking to her sister about the thunderstorm) and the opening of *A Sentimental Journey* (the protagonists' conversation about inheritance laws) has long been noted by scholars researching Wirtemberska's writing and the introduction of Sternean features into Polish literary texts, that is Polish Sterneism.[31] The second direct reference occurs in Chapter Fourteen where an account of the protagonist's walk is preceded by the following narratorial explanation, which moreover connects to that of the author's own footnote:

Such charity collections were, at their most basic level, a type of "sentimental journey" as undertaken by Yorick,* and in which the Reader, if he or she is curious, might accompany Malvina; but if such minute detail, which amuses so pleasantly when portrayed by the wit of Sterne, begins to bore the Reader when executed by the stroke of a weaker pen, she may skip over it without great loss.

* *A Sentimental Journey:* everyone is acquainted with this enjoyable and witty work by Sterne (Wirtemberska's own note). (76)

Malvina contains no more direct references to Sterne. Yet there is much to suggest links between *Malvina* and Sterne's novels in certain compositional elements. These are mainly elements located in the narrative form of the story, as well as in the division of the entire narrative

---

30 This is discussed by Alina Aleksandrowicz in "Polska 'Podróż sentymentalna'", published together with her edition of Wirtemberska's Sternean text, *Niektóre zdarzenia*, Warsaw 1972.

31 This parallel has been noted by Kazimierz Bartoszyński, who uses the Latin formula of *in medias res* to talk about this early novelistic form (1977, 681).

and event-based novelistic material into chapters. Jan Śniadecki also corroborates this view.

The structure of *Malvina* is not at all simple. It features a serpentine, irregular succession of two narrative forms, a broken and complicated course of events, alongside a contrastingly harmonious ordering of this changeable and fluid narrative and event-based material within two volumes, each consisting of fourteen chapters. These structural elements are instrumental in reconciling the event-based and narrative order and disorder, which shows that Wirtemberska had learnt her Sternean lesson well. From this perspective, the most important aspect is the structure, subjected to the dual narrative form of the tale and the letters across the whole of Wirtemberska's novel. This dual form is, as I have tried to demonstrate, a function of the slotting of the regularity in the chapter poetics into the irregularity of the shifts between the tale and the letters.

Wirtemberska's drawing on Sterne's art of disharmonious novelistic composition is also evident in another, more tangible aspect. In *Malvina*, the regular arrangement of chapters, which introduces harmony into the serpentine, irregular "exchanges" between the tale and the letters, is counterbalanced by a certain contradictory quality, which, however, does not preclude the regular arrangement of chapters, defined and accentuated by the Roman numerals. Yet within this arrangement, it corresponds formally to the qualities residing in the shifts between the tale and the letters. This is the serpentine, irregular aspect of the chapter poetics.

The basis for such a contention is the typological variety of chapter headings. The most common ones, which give a name to or explain the events, are interspersed with those which refer to the letters quoted in them or to the properties of the chapters themselves. Let us note that the irregularity in the arrangement of chapters results from the oscillating sequence of themed titles (such as Chapter One: "Thunder and Lightning", or Chapter Three: "In Which the Reader Learns More Clearly Who Malvina Was"), titles containing quotations (such as Chapter Four: "Wanda's Letter to her Aunt") and autothematic titles (such as Chapter Ten: "A Very Brief Chapter").

Among Wirtemberska's chapter titles, the most remarkable and interesting are those which make reference to the very nature of a particular chapter. They also demonstrate Wirtemberska's imitation of Sterne's novelistic structure. Let us note that in Volume One, Chapter Ten is entitled "A Very Brief Chapter"; in Volume Two, Chapter Sixteen is entitled "In Brief", while Chapter Twenty-One – "A Rather Miserable Chapter"; the last chapter in Volume Two, and of the whole novel, is entitled "The

End". The significance of chapters with autothematic titles, which stand out against the rest, consists in their dual nature. Just like other chapters, they present new episodes of the plot. But, unlike others, by means of their titles, they point to themselves as purely novelistic creations, as well as to other chapters as important "tools" for generalising the problems discussed in the novel. The significance of these chapters is mimetic and technical.

The same kind of mimetic and technical significance is attached to the digressive chapters in *Tristram Shandy* as well as to chapters with eccentric titles in *A Sentimental Journey*. Their duality is however more complex. This is mainly because in the chapters of Sterne's two novels, the duality fulfils more functions than in the chapters with autothematic titles in Wirtemberska's novel. In *Malvina*, this mimetic and technical duality serves only the purpose of upholding its existence as a novel. It is no coincidence that the irregular arrangement of chapter titles, among which those very autothematic titles stand out, complements the irregular arrangement of the narrative forms: these are the most important structural properties of *Malvina*. They signal the influence of the authorial and narratorial interpretation of events, thereby illustrating their literary and bookish nature. The mimetic and technical duality of the chapters in *Tristram Shandy* and *A Sentimental Journey*, on the other hand, does not so much serve the overall works themselves as their major elements, from events portrayed to chapters, thus placing them at the centre of more general, genric and formal novelistic issues. In *Tristram Shandy*, this is done by means of digressions, in which such issues are demonstratively pondered by the protagonist as he writes his autobiography. In *A Sentimental Journey*, it is done by means of the peculiarities resulting from the succession of chapter titles that highlight the superiority of the protagonist-traveller's creative inventiveness as he shapes his narrative techniques subjectively – with regard to the objective resources at his disposal. This is why *Tristram Shandy*, within individual chapters, features a condensation of heterogeneous narrative elements: the tale which reports on the events; the interpretative discourse about the tale; philosophical and aesthetic musings, and so on. *A Sentimental Journey*, in turn, features a condensation of subjective narrative elements: the protagonist-traveller's observations and feelings, formulated as carefully as possible in the one mental and writerly manner available.

Ricoeur also stresses that Sterne's great predecessors – Defoe, Fielding and Richardson, exploited the whole store of novelistic conventions to the full. These conventions included those whose "formal suggestiveness" was purposefully concealed in order for the "the aim of 'representing' the reality of life" to come to the fore, with the aim of portraying "the familiar, the ordinary, the everyday". These conventions used "simple and direct language" and were commonly used in the "pseudo-autobiographical" and "epistolary novel" (Ricoeur 1985, 12–13). Ricoeur says:

> Hence to render the texture of daily life as closely as possible was taken to be an accessible and, finally, not problematic task. [...] Everything happened as though only ever more complex conventions could approach what was natural and true (1985, 12–13).

Sterne was the author who combined awareness of tradition at its sharpest, as well as the arbitrariness of the novelistic convention, with his own authorial innovations when it came to the techniques that he himself employed. As a result, readers' experience, conditioned by traditional means of expression, which created an illusion of "natural[ness] and tru[th]" of the presented world (Ricoeur 1985, 13), was complemented by purposefully provoked reader responses, based on revealing the conventionality of the presented world. Ricoeur thus summarises the solutions used in the poetics of the novel which indicate the gap between Sterne and his great predecessors:

> It is no small paradox that it was reflection on the highly conventional character of such novelistic discourse that finally led to the reflection on the formal conditions of this very illusion of proximity and, thereby, led to the recognition of the basically fictive status of the novel itself. (1985, 12)

Ricoeur's more recent discussion of "the metamorphoses of the plot" in the seventeenth- and eighteenth-century English novel corroborates the validity of the interpretative conclusions formulated earlier by the Formalist Shklovsky. Several times Shklovsky problematized issues related to the transformation, in Sterne's novels, of narrative forms typical of the earlier novels by Defoe, Fielding and Richardson.[32] Like Ricoeur, he considers the core of Sterne's art of novel writing to be the art of presentation, which "makes it possible to sense the differences between the things which cannot be sensed" (Shklovsky 1964, 80; trans. from the Polish trans. M.O.). Most probably Shklovsky would have approved of

---

32 Shklovsky did this while the Russian Formalist School flourished, and after its dissolution, in his "Evgenii Onegin" and "The Novel as Parody".

the above statement of Ricoeur's that the previous conventions, which were the subject of Sterne's polemic, achieved the status of "natural[ness] and tru[th]" (Ricoeur 1985, 13). The work by Shklovsky and Ricoeur proves beyond doubt that Sterne succeeded in restating the conventions of novelistic narrative by restoring to them the formal significance of convention.

It is indeed appropriate that the leading motif in Shklovsky's discussions of Sterne's novels is the issue of chapters. In his view, Sterne treated chapters as the core of the novelistic convention. The opposite extreme are those novels where the division into chapters goes barely noticed by readers. In Sterne's novels, the division into chapters was, Shklovsky tells us,

> a method for analysing life's vicissitudes, and at the same time a method for bringing forward the differences between life and art which can no longer be sensed and yet still exist in reality. The narrative division actually aims to create such distinct differences, as well as allows for choosing individual elements out of a whole sequence of events. (1964, 55–56; trans. from the Polish M.O.)

Marian Hobson's conclusions about Sterne's novels are similar to those of Shklovsky and Ricoeur. She discusses the characteristic forms of illusion found in eighteenth-century French art and literature, that is the contemporary ways of situating the presented reality in between fantasy and fake authenticity in the visual and verbal arts. One of the issues Hobson considers is the parallel between Denis Diderot's *Jacques the Fatalist* and Sterne's *Tristram Shandy*.

According to Hobson, the contemporary French novel shaped two forms of illusion. "In both forms the relay of appearance is there, but one form attempts to stabilise it, the other plays with it" (Hobson 1982, 305). Those novels which wanted to demonstrate that they were not novels relying on a form of illusion, aimed at overt elimination of illusion. They used narrative devices designed to achieve verisimilitude, such as letters for instance, in order to present their plots as feasible. This is the case with Rousseau's *Julie, ou la nouvelle Héloïse*. At the opposite end of the spectrum were those novels which openly challenged the illusion. At some points, they paraded themselves as novels; at others, they flatly denied this very possibility. In this way, they left their readers in doubt, on which Hobson comments: "If it is not a novel, is it true?" (Hobson 1982, 129). In Hobson's view, the form of illusion shaped by the latter type of novel ought to be labelled "oscillating" (Hobson 1982, 129). The game played within these novels was aided by the "author-figure" (Hobson 1982, 130). The very presence of this figure made it possible to manipulate the fictional verisimilitude which successfully parades as truth, along with the entire cognitive ambivalence of this situation: "Fictional material is allowed to coalesce, only to be interrupted" (Hobson 1982, 129). *Jacques the Fatalist* and the earlier *Tristram Shandy* are cases in point.

Hobson's explorations, formulated through terminology different from that of Shklovsky and Ricoeur, are a different take on the novelistic conventions of illusion and disillusion, indicated by the other two scholars. In Hobson's terminology, illusion is the problem of "balancing" the interplay between fiction and simulated authenticity. In Shklovsky's and Ricoeur's terminology, it is the problem of the interplay between the apparently natural and the actually formal significance of novelistic conventions. What matters to us most is that Shklovsky, Ricoeur and Hobson all link the emergence of the disturbed illusion in the eighteenth-century English and French novel with the clever inclusion into the novels' plots of the real authors themselves, as is the case with Sterne or Diderot – by making fictional authors the protagonists of these plots. Studies by these three researchers offer one common conclusion. In Sterne's and Diderot's novels, the inclusion of the author figures into the plot converts these very novels into unique manifestations of novelistic story-telling affecting the events described in them. Hobson's observations as she summarises the qualities which differentiate Rousseau's novel from Diderot's (and Sterne's) novel pertain precisely to this shift from illusion conceived as a property of events situated within the novel to illusion which transcends this inner space, questioned on the plane of its novelistic creation:

> Rousseau's *La Nouvelle Héloïse* takes the relations of "illusion" and "reality" as a theme, and bends the relay of appearance into a circle within the confines of the book: the question of the illusive-or-not nature of Julie's experience does not refer out beyond the book, but casts a complex light on the events contained within it. On the other hand, Diderot's *Jacques le fataliste* imbricates appearance: by playing with the relay of the tale within the tale, it forces us to be aware of the flickering nature of what appears. (Hobson 1982, 306)

When I first defined the manner in which the shifts of narrative forms occur in Wirtemberska's novel as an oscillating pattern of the tale and the letters, I had in mind Sterne's nomenclature, which he used to question the straight line as a model for describing real-life and literary events.

The traces of Sterne's novelistic art, visible in the composition of *Malvina,* provide a framework for all other Sternean influences which can be found in this novel. Here I mean not only the female protagonist and her quest, modelled upon Yorick's journey, but also the understanding of the correlations between human emotional lives and ethical assessments and choices, parallel to those in Sterne's writing.[33] This understanding is reflected in the events which make up the episodes of the *Malvina* story. Yet it would be difficult to precisely identify the aspects of these events which bring them closest to Sterne. Primarily, this is because Wirtemberska, when depicting human sensibility and human affections as powerful forces, capable of overcoming moral ambiguity, was equally inspired by Rousseau as she was by Sterne. When enlarging on this Classical, Enlightenment theme, she did so in the spirit of pre-romantic emotionalism.

The Multiplicity of "Twinned" Personal Unities and Dualities

Although *Malvina* as a whole work points to the figure of Maria Wirtemberska as its one and only creative source, in the novel's composition and narration, the figure of the author features as a creative source and is not the one and only: it is, in fact, split into two. There, at the very source, the writer is not only the author of *Malvina,* but also the narrator who plays the part of the novelist, which – to be precise – is a "twinned" division and combination of the two personal incarnations at the same time. In my discussion, I have highlighted the most significant aspect of *Malvina*'s structure and narration, i.e. the alternating irregular pattern of the tale and the letters, and highlighted the most general manifestations of simultaneous interdependency and the disconnectedness of the author and the narrator as Wirtemberska's "twinned" incarnations. This does not, however, exhaust the subject of the "twinned" personal unities and dualities, in which Wirtemberska becomes implicated in her novel. Indeed, the complementariness of the disparate creative acts of the author and the narrator brings more issues to light. These are less general manifestations contributing to the spoken and written narrative, as well as to concrete events. Hence, we must also consider the fact that, in *Malvina,* the "twinned" connections between the author and the narrator, groun-

---

33 The links between emotionalism and moral norms are discussed in detail against the backdrop of Sterne's sentimentalism by Kazimierz Bartoszyński (1977).

ded in the close connection between the spoken and written narrative and the events where letter-writing is instrumental, are multiplied by means of an additional link – the female protagonist herself, Malvina. Both the author and the narrator are linked to her by means of a "twinned" reciprocity. All in all, these "twinned" aspects create a whirlpool of interdependencies and independencies. Such additional observations make it possible to fully understand why I have assumed that personal unity in duality concurrent with personal duality in unity, which is the essence of twindom in literal terms, is the model of personal relationships incorporated into the events presented through the novelistic narrative and into the narrative itself.

"Twinned" connections between the author and the novel's protagonist gain durability thanks to these "twinned" references which, connecting the author with the narrator as they do, at the same time connect the narrator with the protagonist. The character of Malvina emerges out of the narrator's spoken and written discourse, "twinned" with the author's novelistic discourse. "Twinned" connections between the author and the narrator thus express this special state of Wirtemberska's existence which allows her to perceive from the outside (through the narrator's eyes) the course of another person's (the protagonist's) life, while at the same time allowing her to turn this perception into a reflection of her own (i.e. the author's) inner life. It is thanks to this mechanism that in *Malvina* the author faces both the narrator and the protagonist, presented by the narrator, as individuals distinct from herself but, at the same time, created in her own image.

The fact that Wirtemberska names her protagonist "Malvina", the author's own drawing-room pseudonym, is the most spectacular manifestation of what I propose here. In the act of giving the same name to the female protagonist and to the first segment of the novel's title, I see a symbol of the "twinned" connections which bind the narrator and the author to the protagonist of the novel. In consequence, the literary, Ossianic significance of the name of "Malvina", which serves to characterise and single out the female protagonist, becomes enriched with other literary meanings, this time pertaining to a flesh-and-blood individual, Maria Wirtemberska (after: Aleksandrowicz 1978b, 257).

We cannot pinpoint exactly the "twinned" interconnections between the author and the protagonist with as much precision as we can those between the narrator and the protagonist, or between the author and the narrator. Yet because we know that the "twinned" connection between the author and the protagonist comes to the fore through those other "twinned" connections, we can outline the range of its content on this basis.

How is all this done within the novel? To understand this, it is important to view events in a comparative manner, oscillating between two subject sources. It is by following this cognitive directive that both the "twinned" narrator-protagonist and author-protagonist connections emerge. The narrator follows this directive when she opts for telling the story of Malvina's emotional tribulations through passages from her letters or letters by other characters. The same occurs when she develops the story through repeated shifts from issues of personal significance to Malvina and other characters to the presentation of her own views on these issues, or the other way around. This shift from one to another presentational and interpretative perspective becomes the foundation of the "twinned" connections which link her to the protagonist – as does her perception of affairs brought about by the events in a way which interlocks her own "views" about them with the protagonist's "views". The cognitive directive, that is the "twinned" connection between the narrator and the protagonist, becomes simultaneously the foundation of the "twinned" connection between the author and the protagonist. It equips the author with possibilities which, on the strength of this very cognitive principle, are available to the narrator. Hence the narrator is given the opportunity to locate her "twinned" reflection in the protagonist; the author – in the other two. This occurs, in both cases, following the interlocking views of the two "twinned" parties about the matters of importance to them, that is an "exchange of opinion" between them. The author remains the co-creator of the cognitive directive on which the narrator's acts of presentation and interpretation are focused; she also becomes a co-participant in a cognitive performance which has been called into being in this way. The participation of the author counts in this performance no less than that of the narrator, even though it remains somewhat less definite. It pertains to the image which Wirtemberska the author creates of herself – as a person with a rich inner life, and one ready to share the story of what personal experience is. What shapes this image is the content of the "twinned" connections between the author and the protagonist. The reason why it takes on the form of a cognitive performance is that the "twinned" connections between the author and the protagonist are fulfilled through the medium of the "twinned" connections between the narrator and the protagonist.

Before I illustrate this from the novel's material, let me examine the preface to the novel. The preface constitutes a distinct part of the novel

– one in which Wirtemberska presents herself and speaks as the author exclusively. It is significant then that, when pondering the role of reading romances in shaping readers' personal experience, she highlights the role of comparing the components of this cognitive performance, in which the author herself, standing face-to-face with both narrator and protagonist, has participated:

> Whereas in romances, in those faithful portraits, in which almost every reader encounters events similar to those he or she has experienced, emotions familiar to his own heart, errors into which he himself has fallen, passions which he has met often in life, that reader involuntarily becomes caught up in the portrayal, makes comparisons, reflects. And often as a result of those reflections, made without prejudice, the conviction takes root in his heart that whatever his fate, whatever his circumstances, *striving for virtue is a more certain way than any other of striving for happiness.* (3–4; italics original)

Wirtemberska herself could not have been a stranger to the kind of personal experience which she deems typical of reading romances. One of the phrases used at the opening of the quoted description of this complex phenomenon ("almost every reader") testifies to this. Moreover, the precision with which she enumerates the intellectual and moral acts attending the reading of romances suggests that Wirtemberska must have been familiar with them not only as a reader but also as an author. In brief, it implies that she must have considered these acts to be the building material of personal experience not only for the readers of romances, but also for their authors. The very conviction, so aptly rendered by Wirtemberska, that reading romances is an extraordinary personal experience and that it bears fruit in the reality of existence and ethics, demonstrates that those individual acts, thanks to which it is possible to achieve this end result, such as "becom[ing] caught up in the portrayal", "making comparisons" and "reflecting", must have had for her a very real existential and ethical dimension.

The Narrator – Malvina: Closeness, Sympathy, Understanding

The narrator does not hide her closeness to her protagonist. Her attitude reflects her attachment to her protagonist as the image of a person, created by herself, to whom she remains equally close:

> But since the opportunity arises, let me be permitted to give my own, sincere representation of my Malvina and may I be forgiven for lingering a while over this portrait. I admit my weakness for the original, therefore it should not seem strange that I indulge myself a little longer with my description. (26)

The narrator's attitude, full of such positive feeling, makes it possible for her to present and interpret the behaviours, actions and spoken utterances of her protagonist all the more naturally. In other words, it enables her to recognise the protagonist's sensations, which are expressed through these external spheres of activity, all the more naturally. This ability of the narrator parallels the protagonist's ability to portray sensations in her letters. Malvina feels and thinks; the narrator who tells her story and quotes from her letters, sympathises and understands. As a result, the narrator's tale expresses the protagonist in a way different from that expressed by her letters, quoted in the tale: it is less direct, but equally sharp on observation and reflection. This utterly positive effect is achieved not only because the narrator shifts from recounting the protagonist's emotional upheavals to quoting from her letters. Another factor is that, in the tale, she shifts many times from presenting Malvina's sensations, as she recognises them from her external activity, to expounding on her own opinions about these sensations, or the other way around. Were this not the case, the narrator's tale would not equal the protagonist's letters in its wealth of observations and reflections.

Here I point to those properties of the narrator's dual discourse which, apart from all that they carry, make that discourse the common ground of the "twinned" connections between the narrator's person and personality as well as between the person and personality of the protagonist. The syntactic and semantic foundation for this is the narrator's shifting from the tale, featuring the protagonist, to the quoting of the protagonist's own letters, thus making the dual narratorial discourse a field where the two characters and their personalities confront each other. The most important syntactic and semantic expression of this, meanwhile, adding the sense of "twinned" connections" to the confrontations between the narrator and the protagonist, is the narrator's shifting within the tale itself, from the presentation of the protagonist's sensations to the presentation of her own opinion about them, or the other way around – from a depiction of the sensations to the presentation of opinions. Now let me focus on the tale itself as the most significant element of what I wish to outline.

The seemingly "twinned" connections which the narrator forges between herself and the protagonist consist in the establishment of complete reciprocity between them. Yet this is not so when the narrator informs the reader, as in the passages below, about the identical mental states in herself and her protagonist: "In this Malvina thought much like myself" (75) and "I am unable to say, for Malvina herself could not properly understand" (88; see the third and fourth examples below). This is because the narrator's convictions and her recognition of the protagonist's sensations, or – conversely – the protagonist's sensations and the narrator's convictions, cannot be reconciled with each other (see the first, second and third examples). What the narrator recounts, either to begin with or at a later point, as she recognises Malvina's sensations, does not fully correspond to what she has to say about these sensations from her own experience. The result of alternating these two ways of providing information about the protagonist, is that any pure reciprocity between the narrator and the protagonist becomes blurred. This occurs even though the narrator, when shifting in her tale between the two forms of conveying information, establishes "twinned" connections between herself and her protagonist.

The first example:

A bench under a spreading chestnut at the far end of the dike enticed her towards it. The view over the backwater, the wooded knoll, the Vistula, the loveliest of landscapes made this spot especially attractive. Malvina rested there and removed the white veil that had concealed her face. Mechanically she took up her guitar and, having strummed a while to herself, began to sing in a low voice words that reflected her feelings:

> To be loved as one loves
> To find a soul to match one's soul,
> Is it a request too frivolous
> To move the heavenly whole?
>
> Vain dreams of happiness,
> Where hearts deceive the mind,
> Constant, sweet illusoriness,
> No requital will you find!

People are sometimes amazed when infatuated lovers, by some peculiar twist of fate, always contrive to find themselves in the very place where they might catch a glimpse, if only for a moment, of the object of their infatuation. This does not happen by magic and we should stop being surprised by it. It is not difficult to conceive how those who are constantly occupied with the same thought might also, to some degree, act the same. Ludomir, preoccupied exclusively with Malvina, as she was likewise preoccupied with him, had also risen with the dawn, and gone into the garden, so that he might think about her in freedom. Hearing her voice he ran to where she was sitting, unobserved by her. (36–37)

The second example:

Those who imagine that the first moments following a loss are the most painful judge wrongly. Then at least everyone is occupied with the event, talks about it, is involved in it. The person whose loss is mourned is not forgotten, not yet regarded as totally removed and remote. The heart, unaccustomed to grieving, does not admit the thought that grieving is without return; the beginning of the most terrible separation appears to be but a temporary parting. But when days, hours, events follow on one after the other and fail to restore the person who is loved, who is needed, who is missed every day, every moment – oh! Only then do we realise our misfortune and constantly say to ourselves with an aching sigh: "Alas! He really has gone forever!"

In the first moments following Ludomir's disappearance Malvina had, in accordance with her undertaking, sufficient self-control to enable her to listen almost with indifference even to the conversations of her aunt and sister upon the subject.

"It's true," her aunt said on one occasion, "that his concealment of his social position, of his name, this sudden departure, are things which remain unclear, and I have never read anything like them in any romance. But all the same I cannot forget that Malvina owes him her life, and I cannot believe that this same Ludomir, who possessed something particularly noble in his bearing, was nothing but a dissembling imposter."

These last words touched Malvina acutely.

"If that is what he really is," she hurriedly declared, "then I alone should suffer as a punishment for my lack of caution in receiving him into my home. But if he is not, then it would be a cruel injustice to thank him for his efforts during the fire and for saving my life with such wrongful suspicion. So as we are unable to judge his conduct with certainty, it seems to me it would be best to discuss it as little as possible."

These words put a stop to her aunt's talk. In order to comply with Malvina's immediate wishes, and later due to the natural passage of time, everyone at Krzewin first stopped mentioning Ludomir and then stopped thinking about him. This was what Malvina had demanded, this was what she had appeared to want, but when it happened, longing for him intensified sharply. Nothing amused her any longer, nothing distracted her. The dismal autumn that followed in the wake of such a pleasant summer, enveloping all nature in its grey shroud, only increased her desolate melancholy. After several months spent in this mood her health finally began to suffer due to the condition of her spirit. (46–47)

The third example:

Activity may sometimes serve as a substitute for happiness, especially when it embraces a useful end. I do not know if my Readers will share my opinion, but, having experienced so many times the efficacity of this medicine, I would recommend it to anyone. Oppressed sometimes by self-mortification, disheartened by adversity, brought back to my senses from the sweet delusions of my first youth by the sad reality of events, sometimes, I tell you, I would have sunk completely into dangerous depression, had it not been for my love of employment. This love, implanted in my mind by the most welcome advice when I was still in my childhood years, became characteristic of me as I grew up; it enhanced my sunny days and often made bearable the overcast ones. In this Malvina thought much like myself and, having experienced that somewhat incomprehensible and therefore all the more tormenting nostalgia, with which force of circumstances and the chaos of her emotions oppressed her heart, felt less capable of occupying herself at home with work of her own making and seized at the employment which collecting for charity might bring her. To make oneself useful to the poor, to the sick, to destitute old age, to an abandoned child – was the most agreeable nourishment for her tender soul, whilst to step from house to house and take a peep at different pictures of private domestic life would provide an involuntary means of distraction. (75)

The fourth example:

I am unable to say, for Malvina herself could not properly understand, why in her prayers her memories of Ludomir were automatically associated in her thoughts with the memory of the poor (supposed) madman. The limestone hillock beside the Vistula, the white muslin (or so Dżęga assumed it to be) and the unhappy man, for whom it was the only treasure in the world, were engraved constantly on her memory and became involved with her most personal and intimate thoughts. (88)

The above passages demonstrate that the narrator's techniques rely on her juxtaposing and comparing whatever arises from Malvina's personal experience to draw her attention on account of her own personal experience. This occurs both when the narrator stresses that her own and the protagonist's sensations are identical (the second example), and when she does not do that (the other three examples). In both cases however, the foundation of the narrator's attitude towards her protagonist is one of sympathy and understanding, whose essence lies in comparative perceptions and definitions. The interplay of the "twinned" connections, conspicuous in the narrator's tale, depends on her repeated shifts from "vivid" representations of Malvina's sensations to reflections about these sensations. The train of thought which then emerges and determines the tale's progress, makes it possible for the narrator and the protagonist to "reflect" both herself and the other, while at the same time ruling out their complete reciprocity.

This can best be demonstrated in the example below. It contains an account of the protagonist's sensations and a presentation of the narrator's opinions concerning those sensations. Yet, unlike in the previous examples, it contains not two but three separate commentaries by the narrator. The first one is the narrator's matter-of-fact account of Malvina's "grey" days (112), which represent her inner torment. The second is the reflective commentary which elucidates the reasons for this radical change in Malvina's circumstances, contrasting her past enjoyment of "the passing moments with calm indifference", with her now "sw[inging] constantly between extraordinary happiness and unbearable yearning" (113). The narrator's third effusion is an emotional statement of the extremity of sensations related to those aspects of love which bring happiness and those which do not:

The interval of time which elapsed before the return of Prince Melsztyński was, for Malvina, tedious and undistinguished by any interesting coincidence. It was a litany of those grey days which everyone experiences sometime in life and which we watch passing with regret, not because they are happy days, but because they leave no joy or profit behind them.

Malvina had lost her taste for her customary activities, and perhaps for the first time in her life they were unable to keep her occupied. An intolerable restlessness, which she could not explain to herself, drove her constantly from the house. She spent the greater part of the day paying inconsequential and uninteresting visits, returning home in the evening, indescribably bored and exhausted, and then going to bed with the depressing thought that the next day would be just as dull as the one she had only just managed to get through.

Why was it that when she was living at gloomy, lonely Głazów castle, without any amusements, any diversions, and with many a cause for sorrow, Malvina never experienced the oppressive torment of boredom? It is not hard to grasp. At Głazów her young spirit, not yet stirred by passion, was able unperturbed to make good use of every moment, discover a good side to every circumstance and occupy herself with the slightest thing. But since the time she had got to know Ludomir at Krzewin, a new world, so to speak, had opened before her, where she no longer enjoyed the passing moments with calm indifference but swung constantly between extraordinary happiness and unbearable yearning.

One of the worst consequences of love is the fact that once one has experienced its heightened emotions, those emotions take over one's whole being, creating a heaven on earth while they last, but rendering them dead to everything in the world other than themselves, and when they pass, everything seems empty without them, colourless, lacking in purpose, futile. Oh, what a long time is needed once love has expired to recover one's appetite for life! What number of interminable days, how many laborious, insufferable hours one has to get through in order to return to that sweet, unruffled state of tranquillity, to which, alas, despite our toil and striving, it is never possible to return entirely! What then should one do in these circumstances? Never fall in love...? – but that also makes life not worth living! Love...? – and torture oneself all one's life? I myself hold no opinion on this matter, or rather I choose to keep it to myself. Let my Readers judge from their own experience. (112–113)

All three of the narrator's commentaries, of which the quoted passage from the tale is composed, enable the reciprocal reflection in one another of the narrator and the protagonist. The images of Malvina's "unbearable yearning", which the narrator presents in her second utterance, "which she could not explain to herself" (112), give way in the third section to the narrator's reasoning as she grasps Malvina's mental state. Yet the whole individuality of Malvina's "unbearable yearning" is lost within this reasoning. No real or concrete situations are mentioned, as was the case with those used to illustrate Malvina's state of mind in the first effusion. Their place is taken by the narrator's opinions on those aspects of love which make one happy or unhappy, which bring to mind the dilemma regarding the role of suffering in situations where one runs away from love and in others – where one throws oneself into love: "Never fall in love...? – but that also makes life not worth living! Love...? – and torture oneself all one's life?" (113).

Yet although these reflections by the narrator do not include any circumstances related to Malvina's personal situation, they are conveyed through discourse which bears traces of that other language, which sets out to name individual manifestations of the protagonist's mental torment. These traces are the phrases, in the narrator's language of reasoning, which make more precise the essence of the crisis brought about by an end to love in human life. These phrases are synonymous with those which, in the narrator's first effusion, are used to refer to the change experienced by Malvina because of the lack of Ludomir's love. The time when love ends is depicted as "colourless, lacking in purpose, futile" (113). To Malvina, Ludomir's absence, in turn, represents "those grey days which [...] leave no joy or profit behind them", "inconsequential and uninteresting visits" and "indescribabl[e] bored[om] and exhaust[ion]" (112). The narrator's synonyms, although they manage to give a name to what has already been given a name, do not repeat what has already been said – they are in fact elements of another outpouring.

It is this correspondence in the content described synonymically that unifies the protagonist's sensations with the narrator's thoughts, at the same time separating the two spheres. It is a tangible sign of how the narrator and the protagonist, as one and the same person and personality, and simultaneously as two different persons and personalities, reflect each other. Here, the performance of the "twinned" connections takes place between youth and maturity, between the known and the unknown, a dream and its fulfilment, an expectation of happiness and an understanding of happiness.

The narrator's second effusion illustrates this point. On the one hand, before the narrator explains the whole thing further on, she communicates to the reader that love is the cause of Malvina's "unbearable yearning" (113). On the other hand, this outpouring enables the narrator to pass on to a form of reasoning, which reveals the fundamental dilemma of the lovers. Moreover, the middle section does not only inform the reader of the protagonist's sensations, but also gives vent to the narrator's convictions. In so doing, it illustrates on the microlevel the "twinned" interplay between the two persons and personalities, which – more generally – is enacted on the shared ground of all three effusions, and – still more generally – within the space of the entire tale of which these effusions are a part.[34]

---

34 The narrator's effusion, which echoes the protagonist's "internal" monologue may well be viewed as an example of so-called free indirect discourse. I have not used this term on purpose as I wish to make a connection between this remarkable utterance by the narrator, in some

At this point, the question arises: What are, to the narrator, the "twinned" connections between herself and the protagonist? My answer is: To the narrator, they carry existential and creative meaning. They are elements of her dual discourse, in which – let us remember – the tale is combined with the protagonist's letters and the letters of other characters. The essence of these connections lies in the protagonist's and narrator's analogous mental acts, as a result of which the former's personal experience is translated into the latter's personal experience. Both to Malvina, whose letters document her emotional turmoil, and to the narrator, who recounts this turmoil and quotes from Malvina's letters, personal experience is something that they both capture and make precise through their efforts of feeling and thinking. In the case of Malvina, who responds in the epistolary – that is, in a sense, natural – manner, feeling and thinking lead to her continuing recognition of the meanings of facial expressions, deeds and utterances of the two personal incarnations of the man whom she loves. In the case of the narrator, who spins the novelistic tale about Malvina and who quotes from Malvina's letters, that is – who reacts less naturally, the protagonist's feeling and thinking lead to sympathy with Malvina and understanding of Malvina's sensations. This particular way of responding with sympathy and understanding to feeling and thinking makes the narrator perceive Malvina's person and personality through the lens of her own person and personality, and the other way around – that is, perceiving herself and her own personality through the lens of Malvina's person and personality: in a word, it makes her perceive herself as, simultaneously, Malvina and not-Malvina. Had the narrator not engaged in this interplay of "twinned" connections between herself and the protagonist, the dual discourse consisting of the tale and the letters would not have emerged as the novel's most important element, involving as it does the efforts of both the narrator and the author.

---

places reflecting the protagonist's thoughts, and in others – her language, and the creative assumptions unique for this (and no other) narrator.

The Author – (The Narrator) – Malvina: Understanding the Thoughts and Feelings Contained in the Tale, the Letters and the Protagonists' Speech and Writing

The "twinned" connections between the author and Malvina are initiated, as I have already indicated, through the medium of the "twinned" connections between the narrator and Malvina. The two are and are not the same. Each embodies an outcome of Wirtemberska's other personal incarnations. In those "twinned" connections, Wiremberska figures not as herself, but is turned rather into a reflection of herself – into the narrator who makes the connection with Malvina in her novelisticly stylised discourse. Meanwhile, she initiates these "twinned" connections herself by writing a novel from which, in an illusive way, emerges the narrator's storytelling and epistolary discourse, centred on Malvina. In this novel, entitled *Malvina, or the Heart's Intuition*, the "twinned" connections between the narrator and Malvina are closely tied to those linking Malvina with the author. Yet the fact that the two types of "twinned" connections are (and are not) the same is the foundation for the cognitive performance in which Wiremberska becomes involved in her novel. This performance is a special game of Wiremberska's consciousness as author inscribed in her novel.

I have already pointed out that Wiremberska's giving her own drawing-room name to her novel's protagonist is the most telling testimony to the "twinned" connections between the protagonist and herself as author. But I have also pointed out that while this may indeed be telling, it is by no means the only available evidence. In her "twinned" connections with Malvina, Wiremberska as author remains first and foremost the co-creator (in addition to the narrator) of the cognitive approach according to which both interpret the emotional dilemma experienced by the protagonist. This approach, let us remember, allows for the emergence of a mental union between two persons, tracing the interlocking of those persons' "views" about the matters that concern them; tracing what concerns them in a comparative way; following their contemplation of matters equally valid to both. It enables the narrator to find her "twinned" reflection in Malvina, and the author co-creating this approach – in both the narrator and in Malvina. It is striking that the author, having an opportunity to confront both the narrator and Malvina, enters the latter's situation as she faces the two doppelgänger-twinned Ludomirs. *Malvina, or the Heart's Intuition*, the novel, when viewed from this perspective, appears to be the result of Wirtemberska's fulfilment of this confrontative task, parallel to the protagonist's confrontative effort.

In terms of the above, the most significant aspect is that Wirtemberska the author, while adopting the same cognitive approach as her narrator, establishes her "twinned" connection with Malvina in a way different from her narrator's. Wirtemberska the narrator builds that connection, as we recall, thanks to the quotations from Malvina's letters, which enrich her narrative, and thanks to her sympathy for and understanding of the protagonist's sensations, expressed in the tale, which Malvina herself expresses through utterances, behaviours and precisely her letters. Wirtemberska the author in turn builds her "twinned" connection with Malvina thanks to her understanding both of the protagonist's epistolary utterances and of the narrator's reflections and, consequently, thanks to the formation of semantic correspondences between these two perceptions of the protagonist's personal experiences and her own perception of them relayed in the novel's discourse.

The acts of Wirtemberska the author, the understanding and formation of semantic correspondences, are central to several major issues. It is through them that Wirtemberska co-creates, together with the narrator, the cognitive approach which brings both face to face with Malvina. And it is thanks to these acts that *Malvina* the novel, taking on the illusionary appearance of a story-telling and epistolary discourse that includes the letters themselves, remains a sign of Wirtemberska's involvement in it as a cognitive performance, in which she is confronted with her narrator and her protagonist. A major role in shaping these issues is played by the relational nature of the two acts: of understanding and of forming semantic correspondences. Understanding refers here to the knowledge of Wirtemberska the author both about what her protagonist makes of her personal experiences and about what the narrator makes of them: this is what accounts for the duality – the understanding of understanding. In the hands of Wirtemberska the author, the creation of semantic correspondences becomes a subtle tool for finding a separate and unique semantic expression for the epistolary and story-telling forms of the protagonist's personal experience; and also, indirectly, for expressing the experience itself. It is this relational nature of both acts that gives the connections between the author and the narrator and Malvina the aspect of mirror reflections of one another, and their partial reciprocity. In this way, it gives to these connections the same meaning which was given by the narrator to her sympathy with, and understanding of, Malvina's sensations. With the reservation, however, that in that case the locus of self-reflection and partial reciprocity of the participants lies in the narrator's discourse; here the process centres around the author's intellectual acts as they become elements of her novel. These acts, focused on the endeavours of understanding and forming semantic correspondences, enable the author to grasp, in the one and only way possible – that is, based on the novelistic discourse – the internal connections between the many detailed observations, confessions and opinions conveyed by the protagonist's letters, and the corresponding detailed observations, confessions and opinions conveyed by the narrator's story-telling and epistolary discourse in relation to the protagonist's experiences. So when Wirtemberska the narrator establishes a "twinned" connection with Malvina through utterance, at the same time Wiremberska the author parallels it with intellectual acts, from which a unique semantic perception of the protagonist's personal experience emerges. That does not mean, however, that the "twinned" connection set up by Wirtemberska the author between herself and Malvina does not include material which the author was unable to put into words. It only means that this content springs from her acts of understanding and forming semantic correspondences, and cannot be defined in a manner as precise as the material which informs the connections between the narrator and the protagonist.

These acts give meaning to the novel's title, to chapter titles, to the motto, to the subject matter of the preface and to the theme of "the heart's intuition" with its novelistic, irregular structure. Briefly speaking, this is an interpretation of personal experience, which draws on a study of the protagonist's psychological and moral sensitivity manifest in her letters and in the narrator's story-telling and epistolary discourse, and expresses the results of that study through the subject matter and structure of the novel. The point is that the written discourse, that is *Malvina* the novel, asserts its supremacy by means of the illusion of speech and writing.

Let us note that all these aspects, including the involvement of Wirtemberska's authorial and narratorial selves in their "twinned" connections with the protagonist, along with other configurations, such as Wirtemberska's involvement in the "twinned" connections with the protagonist through the parallel connections between herself and the narrator, are enacted on the basis of interlocking, or put more literally – of the internal interplay between the spoken and written semantic properties of the novel's discourses. In addition, this process comprises links between the spoken aloud and written utterances of the novel's protagonists. This leads to the conclusion that the true agent of Wirtemberska's "twinned" involvement under discussion is in fact the "twinned" nature of the spoken and written semantic properties that define the discourses making up the novel, as well as defining the protagonists' utterances that form part of the discourses.

Let us also note that within the "twinned" contrasts and correspondences visible within the narrator's discourse, which combines the tale and the letters, as well as within the "twinned" tensions and connections emerging between the protagonists' spoken and written utterances, Wirtemberska the author's acts of understanding and forming semantic correspondences are fulfilled. It is these acts, after all, which enable all these spoken and written elements to surface as illusive elements in the written nature of the novel.

In order to highlight the issues and processes outlined here, I should now return to all the unique properties, analysed above, which accompany the combination of the tale and the letters in the narrator's discourse, as well as situating this spoken and written discourse within the written discourse of the novel. This is not possible, for understandable reasons. So much so, I would like us to bear in mind that we are talking about aspects and processes spawned by a whole subtle range of simultaneous similarities (parallels) and differences (contrasts), both between the spoken status of the tale and the written status of the letters, and the spoken and written status of the novelistic discourse. The creation of these "between" spaces, firstly, is the creation of the form of the tale which stands in contrast to the letters – a transmission that relies on the stylised and real novel-writing acts of the author and the narrator, and yet is endowed with the meaning of an utterance. Secondly, it is also the creation of the story-telling and epistolary discourse, which remains at one and the same time in accord and discord with the novel's written discourse. In short, the creation of the "between" spaces becomes the creation of the illusion of speech and writing, as well as of the semantic impact of the novel. In other words, this is the formation of the mirror relationships which encompass the author, the narrator and the protagonist. This leads me to believe that it is in these spoken and written semantic properties of the discourses making up *Malvina*, as well as in the novel's plot complexities focused around the spoken and written utterances of the protagonists, that the climax of the "twinned" semantic qualities of the voice and the writing is located. Therefore, we should say that it is not so much the "twinned" interplay between the spoken and written semantic properties of the discourses, but the "twinned" semantic energies of the voice and the writing contained within them, that splits and simultaneously sustains the unity of the person of Wirtemberska as author. It should also be said that this semantic energy of the voice and of the writing is what implicates Wirtemberska in the cognitive performance, confronting her with the narrator and with the protagonist – as images of herself and not of herself at the same time.

For Wirtemberska the author, the "twinned" connections that bind her to Malvina, just like the others that bind her in her capacity as narrator to the protagonist, carry existential and creative significance, yet different in kind since she is also a flesh-and-blood individual. These connections are less conspicuous than the others. On the one hand, they are a focus for Wirtemberska's ultimate knowledge of the illusory nature of the novelistic endeavour, which she creates in her capacity as narrator; on the other, they enable her to co-create this narratorial representation of Malvina's tribulations and inner life according to her own knowledge. Even though the content of these connections cannot be specified as accurately as that of the others, which are the subject of the bonds between the narrator and the protagonist, their general nature can be identified. First and foremost, it can be done on the basis of her truly authorial contribution to the novel's creation, evident in its subject matter, structure and the content of the preface. Further, on the basis of that "twinned" situation binding the narrator and the protagonist, but reflected in the one under discussion. And, last but not least, on the basis of the name "Malvina" given to the protagonist. I believe that this very gesture symbolises the material with which Wirtemberska the author fills the "twinned" connections between herself and her protagonist. It is significant that she bestows on her protagonist not her real name, but her drawing-room pseudonym. In this way, naming becomes a means in the same interplay that she maintains with the protagonist in the novel, primarily through her other narratorial incarnation. The naming of her protagonist "Malvina" points to an "affinity" between Malvina and Wirtemberska herself, but – once again – what comes to the fore, as in the novel, is the other "drawing-room" self of the author.

It should be assumed that the most important factor in the "twinned" connections binding Wirtemberska the author to Malvina is the author's attitude to the "events", "errors" and "passions" (4), which she experiences herself, and as a result of which she acquires her familiarity with the most common personal experiences. In her preface to *Malvina*, Wirtemberska says that no one is exempt from these "events", "errors" and "passions" (4), and that novels, by representing such experiences, enable readers to better understand their own personal experience. There is no doubt that these "twinned" connections cover both the experiences of the novel's heroine, related to the emotional dilemma which she needs to resolve, as well as to the author's own inner struggles, victories and failures. All the same, the appearance of the novel's heroine necessitates the disappearance of the character who resembled her, along with the appearance of the one to whom the creation of this character is illusively ascribed. Nothing remains more mysterious than this process, always the same and always inscrutable, which transforms reality into illusion, the author into the narrator, and Maria – into Malvina. If the author's personal experience, with its "events", "errors" and "passions" (4), is the real agent, it has become dissipated. What is at stake then, in the "twinned" connections construed by Wirtemberska the author and binding her to Malvina, is the very possibility for Wirtemberska to reflect herself in her heroine's tribulations and sensations, and not the establishment of event-based parallels between their inner lives. When placing these "twinned" connections at the core of her novel, making them its *spiritus movens*, thereby taking them beyond the bounds of her own consciousness, Wirtemberska illustrates the paradoxical nature of human personal experience, which is perceptible to individuals only through references to matters which bind them to others. The "twinned" connections which the narrator establishes in her storytelling and epistolary discourse are subordinated to the same goal. In this sense, the "twinned" connections established by the narratorial and authorial incarnations of Maria Wirtemberska make up a representation of personal experience which is never entirely individualistic.

148

Part Four
Malvina and the Salon

> Malvina asked Ludomir (who amongst other things reads
> wonderfully) whether he would like to read us *Ludgarda*,
> an original and unconventional tragedy, which has
> recently been published. Ludomir read magnificently,
> with great attention; he seemed to read the scenes not
> only with his eyes but with his heart. (23–24)

Alina Aleksandrowicz has found that Wirtemberska's salon resembled in
its internal organisation and in the cultural and social activities it pursued,
the seventeenth-century salon of the Marquise de Rambouillet, and was
in a sense intended to commemorate its predecessor (Aleksandrowicz,
1974; Aleksandrowicz, 1978b). When discussing seventeenth-century
French salons, and particularly Rambouillet's "blue hotel", the model
for all salons of those and later times, scholars Roger Picard, Roger
Lathuillère and Yuri Lotman present them as specialised institutions
which fulfilled major cultural functions. The salon of the Marquise de
Rambouillet, a select and initiated community of literary people and artists, acted as a counterbalance to the Académie française, the central and
official institution of culture, founded by Cardinal Richelieu. The salon
aimed at creating a cultural reality distinct from and independent of the
state's absolutism, instilling it with refinement and idealism as purifica-
tion from ordinariness and the dictates of political reality (Lotman 1992).
Lotman says, "That opposition was not political: the state's seriousness
was counterbalanced by play; official poetic genres – by personal ones;
the male dictatorship – by a women's state; a national unification – by
a closed system, different from the rest of the world" (1992, 23; trans.
M.O.).
    De Rambouillet's salon, just as much as other similar institutions,
including the salons of Mademoiselle de Scudéry and Madame de La

Fayette, contributed to the shaping of *préciosité*, a complex style which influenced both the writing of literature and social behaviours. The *préciosité* style required nobility and dignity, along with elegant and ornamented language. Lathuillère explains that this style was the focal point for several contradictory tendencies: "on the one hand, it is characterised by purism, concerned with delicacy and good manners; on the other, it aims at a rich expression, a brilliant language, an ornate style" (1966, 679; trans. M.O.).

The complexity of the phenomenon of *préciosité* also resulted from its combining a tendency towards idealism with acknowledgement of the superiority of the human mind. When discussing this self-contradictory aspect of *préciosité*, Lathuillère claims: "passionately concerned with ideal values, it manifests itself as aristocratism that recognizes only one superiority, that of the spirit" (1966, 677; trans. M.O.). Lathuillère believes that the complexity of *préciosité*, cultivated in the French salons of the seventeenth century, made it possible for apparently unconnected phenomena to emerge. They included the idealised and mythologised sentimentality of pastoral romances such as Honoré d'Urfé's *L'Astrée* or Madeleine de Scudéry's *Clélie*, reflection on the old and new French vocabulary by Dominique Bouhours, an insightful analysis of the moral contradictions between desire and marital obligations in Madame de La Fayette's *La Princesse de Clèves*, and eventually the moral and psychological depth of La Rochefoucauld's *Maxims*. In discussing the complexity of *préciosité* and the richness of the contemporary salon culture, Lathuillère lists these issues in precisely this order (1966, 677–678).

Lotman considers "the main property of seventeenth-century French salons to be the blurring of borders between life, play and art" (1992, 25; trans. M.O.). Lathuillère links to them manifestations of a subtle, continuing interplay between real life and the beautifying imagery of poetry and novels. In his opinion, the most common desire driving frequenters to seventeenth-century French salons and to the game itself was to exchange "daily monotony and greyness" for "aspiring to live to the highest degree and in an exaggerated manner" [tenter de vivre au superlatif et dans l'hyperbole] *(*Lathuillère 1966, 339–347; trans. M.O.). Gérard Genette is therefore right to claim that d'Urfé's novel *L'Astrée*, one of those texts which inspired the salons' discourse, salon forms of emotional sensitivity and pseudonyms, ought to be treated "not only as a 'literary genre', but also as a form of sensibility and existence" (1964, 8; trans. M.O.).

The salons discussed by Lathuillère and Lotman were the sites of remarkable complementariness, when it came to human behaviour – the interplay between reality and idealism, the sources of which were literary. Lotman explains:

> Literary texts were written or improvised in a variety of situations, and they were an inseparable part of human lives, while the lives themselves merged with poetic themes. Literary masks came to characterise individuals and define their behaviours in real life. (1992, 25; trans. M.O.)

Yet this transformation of the real salon space into "the world of artistic utopia" was by no means complete:

> Politics and Reason that enlightened it were opposed by Play and Fancy. Yet reason was not expelled: the world of *préciosité* is not the world of some Baroque, tragic folly. It merely follows the dictates of masquerade travesty which ruled the salons. (1992, 24; trans. M.O.)

The literary activity of the salons was most frequently expressed in love and occasional poetry, pastoral and antique tales, epigrammatic genres, portraits and letters. All these various forms of literary activity originated from salon life. It bred the enhanced (in their salon eccentricity) intellectual and ludic uses of these forms. The essence of salon literary activity lay not only with individual artists but also with the community of recipients. Authors used the conventionally concealed "live address" in their works, while the recipients decoded these texts and complemented them with their own creative activity and knowledge, "the communal memory".

It is significant in this respect that the seventeenth-century French salons produced unique forms of their communal pursuits. The major ones which scholars have identified include conversation and correspondence, transformed in the salons into "the art of conversation" and "the epistolary art", as well as adaptations of selected literary themes, improvisations on major social events or competitions for the so-called "bouquets of poems". These activities were aimed, respectively, at focusing the attention of the salon community on particular subjects, and imposing on them the requirements for spontaneity or rivalry. In addition, the literary forms which regularly triggered creative activity in the salon communities also included literary and language games, whose major component was giving the salon frequenters opportunities to demonstrate their intellectual and verbal cleverness: "ingenuity, reflexion and powers of association" (Aleksandrowicz 1974, 13; trans. M.O.). These forms linked the literary texts produced in the salons to the elaborate, unconventional behaviours of the salon attendees. Yet each form taken in isolation made it possible for shared aspects of the salon life to take a different direction. This is why Lathuillère discusses these forms in two distinct ways: jointly – throughout his exhaustive study – as manifestations of the salon culture of the *préciosité* period; and in isolation – when he devotes separate discussions to each individual form in the final chapters of his book.

From its seventeenth-century predecessor, the Hôtel de Rambouillet, and other eighteenth-century model salons, Wirtemberska's salon inherited the tradition of the privileged, communal participation of artists, writers and other people of culture in intellectual life. This was despite the largely democratised (since the seventeenth century) access to products of the intellect. Equally important to the heritage taken up by Wirtemberska's salon, apart from the perpetuation of the fundamental goals of such institutions, were the direct references to the internal structure of the Hôtel de Rambouillet, as well as to the literary texts written in the salon alongside literary and linguistic pastimes. When discussing the "structure" of the Hôtel de Rambouillet, Alina Aleksandrowicz stresses the regularity of the meetings held at Wirtemberska's salon, the choice of Saturdays as meeting days, and the reference to those Saturdays as "blue". The colour blue was in fact the symbol of the Hôtel de Rambouillet. Aleksandrowicz believes that references to the creative pursuits of the Hôtel de Rambouillet can be seen in the way that the frequenters of Wirtemberska's salon indulged in pastimes, such as writing poetry which "belonged to the *jeu de l'amour* convention" (1974, 15; trans. M.O.); writing essays on semantics devoted to the shades of meaning of selected Polish synonyms and antonyms; organizing dedicated parlour games ("secrétaire, riddles, charades, logographs, tales on a set word or poems with the use of set rhymes" (1974, 13; trans. M.O.), which aimed at playful "testing" of the properties of Polish semantics and syntax (1974, 13). Aleksandrowicz stresses that all these pursuits, vital to Wirtemberska's salon, were also affected by local and topical inspirations. She claims, however, that inspirations taken from the types of poetry written and parlour games pursued at the Hôtel de Rambouillet, as well as the structure and symbolism of that French salon, were clearly features of the salon established by Wirtemberska.

Aleksandrowicz believes that all the poetry produced in Wirtemberska's salon followed the *jeu de l'amour* convention, was not "meant for publication" or "wider circulation", and only served the purpose of "literary pastimes of *homo ludens*" (1974, 8–9; trans. M.O.). Yet these texts were collected and preserved by Wirtemberska herself in a manuscript titled *Błękitne soboty zebrane w roku 1808* [Blue Saturdays Collected in 1808] (Aleksandrowicz, 1978b). These are poems whose principal subject is love, placed against a backdrop of other intellectual experiences, which explains their largely antithetical structure. Their titles are telling on this score: "Love and Indolence", "Love and Indifference", "Love and Jealousy" or "Love and Friendship". This poetry, Aleksandrowicz claims, originated from two tendencies. On the one hand, it demonstrated the persistence of the poetic conventions of seventeenth-century French salons, which consisted in the presentation of love, its various kinds and signs. On the other hand, this poetry was an expression of the dominant, new sentimental attitudes, which brought the theme of love once again to the fore.

Synonyms were a frequent motif of both the "inquisitive" reflection on language, as practised in Wirtemberska's salon, and of the parlour games which were enjoyed there. Participants sought and described the different alternations of Polish synonyms, such as, for instance, Ustroić [Ornament] – *Ozdobić* [Decorate] – *Okrasić* [Embellish]; *Gibkie* [Supple] – *Giętkie* [Flexible] – *Sprężyste* [Bouncy]; *Zadumanie* [Reverie] – *Zamyślenie* [Contemplation] – *Smutek* [Sadness];[35] they also played at homonyms and antonyms. In her salon, synonyms were studied by Wirtemberska herself, Ludwik Kropiński, Ignacy Potocki, Tadeusz Matuszewicz and J. M. Fredro.

In Wirtemberska's salon, the preoccupation with Polish synonymy, as was the case with the poetry produced there, was driven by historical and topical concerns. On the one hand, the study of semantic differences between synonyms and the turning of this process into a game harked back to the tradition developed by the French *préciosité* salons. On the other hand, this semantic work and play were a response to the appeal from the Warsaw Learned Society, concerning the compilation of *A Dictionary of Polish Synonyms*. Historically speaking, Aleksandrowicz suggests that one of the major motifs of this salon-based tradition was "to analyse the properties of the dictionary, to qualify the terminology, particularly that referring to the semantics of emotions" (1974, 15; trans. M.O.). As for topical issues, she claims that the contemporary interest in synonymy, as demonstrated by the scholarly society and Wirtemberska's salon,

---

35 Alina Aleksandrowicz has collected texts devoted to synonymy, produced in Wirtemberska's salon (1974; 1978b).

was part of a broader intellectual trend spreading among aristocratic and townsfolk circles, geared towards the popularisation of the Polish language, learning correct Polish usage and expanding users' Polish language competence. In this way the phenomenon of synonymy reconciled the cultural tradition with current cultural challenges.

All this occurred after Polish society and the Polish state had lost their independence and liberty, which is what gave these initiatives a clearly patriotic slant. Besides the Dictionary of Polish Synonyms, another enterprise supported by the Warsaw Learned Society, was Bogumił Linde's Dictionary of the Polish Language. Unlike Linde's dictionary, the study of synonyms was never written, and only parts of it were completed (1974, 15–18).[36] Remnants of these parts are preserved in the essays on synonyms produced in Wirtemberska's salon.

Aleksandrowicz claims that these essays would not have made their way into a dictionary-type publication. They were in fact "fully-fledged literary works", not dictionary entries. Even though they aimed at dictionary-style explication of selected synonyms, they more accurately reflective and lyrical texts on the meanings of selected vocabulary items. It is not conciseness and matter-of-factness but excess and emotionalism that inform the poetics of Wirtemberska's salon's essays on synonyms. "The focus shifts from the external description of the state of affairs to an emotional assessment of the presented issues" (1974, 21; trans. M.O.). Aleksandrowicz is right in saying that, in these essays, the explications of semantic fields of synonyms became demonstrations of the emotional stance of the person who authored the explications. To prove this, she quotes from Kropiński's discussion of the synonyms *Smutek* [Sadness] – *Żal* [Sorrow] – *Rozpacz* [Despair] and Wirtemberska's discussion of *Gibkie* [Supple] – *Giętkie* [Flexible] – *Sprężyste* [Bouncy]:

Sadness. Sorrow. Despair. These are the foes to human happiness and peace of mind. They keep meandering for ever along the paths of our lives! Pure coincidence and destiny rule them, and tell them which heart they are to enter!

Sadness and his entourage keep circling around us every day: regret, ailment, worries, pain, nuisance and dreariness are his attendants. Like midges, they come upon a human being in hordes, and after they have been driven away by joy, cheerfulness, distractions, possibly even happiness, they keep coming back. The figure of Sadness is full of sensibility, his gaze is tearful, his breaths are sighs: he likes friendship, and in her lap she wipes away his tears!

---

36 In this respect, the most influential was Kazimierz Brodziński's "Synonima polskie" (1874).

Sorrow comes from some enormous loss, particularly of a person dear to us... The lightning of unhappiness which strikes the heart first arrests all human faculties, this is when the voice of friendship begins to ail, the voice of pity becomes unbearable, and both work to increase still more the streams of tears!

But what sadness or sorrow can compare with despair!

Suppleness projects an image of subtle elegance, flexibility – of a nice bend, bounciness – of a comparable rebound. The supple outline of the viburnum shrub may compare to a flowy reed swayed by the wind! Flexible twigs of the birch tree sweep over that grave so gently! The bouncy movement of the chest often gives away to inner sorrow or joy.

Bounciness excels at dancing. Suppleness appears the quality of the earliest youth! Flexibility can be used in a moral sense, when it is said: "That man is flexible in his dealings; he is fickle-minded. (1974, 21; trans. M.O.)

The above discussion of synonyms pertains to those studied in Wirtemberska's salon. What is needed, however, is a closer look at this particular, salon-specific attitude to synonyms from the perspective of contemporary linguistics: this will help understand the reasons why the frequenters of the sentimental salon singled out synonymy from among the many other linguistic phenomena.

It is symptomatic that synonyms are treated in twentieth-century linguistics as a field in which language reveals subjectively defined meanings. John Lyons, an expert on meaning in language, tells us that synonyms are used when demonstration is required that words "might have the same referential meaning, but differ in emotive meaning: e.g. 'horse' and 'steed'" (1977, 175). Lyons goes on to say that definition of synonyms relies on the skill to provide "[t]he opposition between a more central, or stylistically neutral, component of meaning and a more peripheral, or subjective, component of meaning" (1977, 175). He continues: "it is not infrequently conflated with the distinction [...] between descriptive and social or expressive meaning" (1977, 175). That said, Lyons refers his readers to his earlier analysis where he declared: "we define expressive meaning [...] to be that aspect of meaning which 'covaries with characteristics of the speaker' [...] and social meaning to be that aspect which serves to establish and maintain social relations" (1977, 51).

It would seem that the literary interpretation of synonyms, carried out by the frequenters of Wirtemberska's salon, in revealing the emotional stances of their authors, reflected the most profound aspect of this linguistic phenomenon. Hence the subjective by nature, "literary" rather than "dictionary" properties of the meaning, demonstrated by synonymous sequences in language communication. Let us note that the wish to express what agitates the speaker at a particular moment, as well as the wish to express through their utterance individuated, subjective messages, usually determine the choice of this and not any other element in a sequence of synonymous words. Synonyms are a "specialised" linguistic means guarding the coherence of our speech and our intentions. This is the reason why, when wishing to express themselves precisely, the speaker is forced to choose between words such as, for instance, "sadness", "sorrow" and "despair". The properties which distinguish the descriptions proposed by participants in the meetings held in Wirtemberska's salon, that is subjectivity, emotionalism or literariness, are deeply rooted in the nature of synonyms as such. It has always been the task of professional lexicographers to objectify these emotive properties. Lyons points out clearly that this work draws upon subtle differences between "more central, or stylistically neutral" and "more peripheral, or subjective" (1977, 175) constituents of meaning. This work continues under the auspices of subjectivity, emotionalism and literariness.

Reading Aloud: A Form of Literary Reception which Internally Binds the Written Word with the Live Voice

Literary salons promoted behaviours which bound together internally the written word and the live voice. In this respect, Wirtemberska's salon was no different from its seventeenth- and eighteenth-century predecessors or other contemporary Warsaw salons.[37] The literary texts originating in the salons were largely limited to poetry, which was read aloud. It assumed two different forms, the written and the spoken, linked to each other through readings or declamations. Therefore, it may be said that, in the salons, purely "literary" qualities were achieved both through writing and by means of the voice – through speech, often with the use of acting, singing or musical techniques. This was fostered by treating the act of literary creation and the act of its literary reception in particular ways which allowed each act to co-exist alongside the other, or possibly

---

37 Andrzej Guzek's entry on "literary salons" contains a discussion of Warsaw's literary salons (Wirtemberska's included) of the eighteenth and the turn of the nineteenth century (1977, 633–638).

even together: in the "performances" of reading, recitations, improvisations, discussions, and the like. The "literary" quality achieved through writing also extended to the epistolary correspondence which arose in the salons and around them. Meanwhile, the "literary" quality achieved through the voice, apart from re-enacting literary texts through readings aloud or declamations, extended to conversation and language games.

Naturally, this does not mean that the attendees of literary salons did not cultivate private reading. Yet the shared, communal nature of salon life privileged spoken reception of literary texts. Hence the literary text could be fulfilled, along with the acts of its reception, in exaggerated, "theatrical" dimensions, which placed authors and recipients in the roles of actors and spectators.

In the seventeenth-century French salons, depicted by Lathuillére and Lotman, spoken forms of literary reception became the focus of idealisational games. They consisted in communal re-articulation of the metaphorical and symbolic content of literary texts within the salon community, instead of relying on individual ideas of this content, as formed by particular members of these communities. When in seventeenth-century French salons people impersonated literary characters or assumed literary names and surnames, this was a symptom of the idealisational attitudes predominating in those circles. Aleksandrowicz has found that the life of Wirtemberska's salon also had its "leitmotifs", which – if not purely idealisational – were certainly aimed at stylisation. The modelling of her salon on the Hôtel Rambouillet was in itself this kind of act. Aleksandrowicz also points out that the poetry writing which occurred in Wirtemberska's salon stylised the community as "a medieval court of love" (1974, 12; trans. M.O.). It is also noteworthy that the participants of the salon meetings and the salonnière herself all assumed names of literary origin.

The spoken forms of literary reception determined the directions and depth of the salon literary games. Naturally, during the two centuries that elapsed between the salon of the Marquise de Rambouillet and that of Princess Wirtemberska, forms of spoken literary reception and the resulting parlour games had both been subject to transformation. All the same, the models of the two pursuits were perpetuated.

An interesting perspective on these issues is provided by Roland Barthes' discussion of the historical processes by which the "writing" became isolated from the "reading". He claims that one major step in this process was, on the one hand, the weakening of the impact of rhetoric as "the great literary code" (1977, 162) of European cultures; and on the other, the growth within these cultures of the impact of professional interpreters of literature, to whom the public would transfer their own role-playing responsibilities when it came to understanding literature, music and painting. Barthes calls this transitional period between Classicism and Romanticism the time of "practising amateurs" (1977, 162). It seems that his statements concerning the contemporary reception of music can be extended to the contemporary reception of literary texts: "there was a period when practising amateurs were numerous (at least within the confines of a certain class) and 'playing' and 'listening' formed a scarcely differentiated activity; then two roles appeared in succession" (Barthes 1977, 162–163). This connection may well be justified: only a couple of lines earlier Barthes points to textual games as intermediaries, in his view, in the process of distancing the writing from the reading:

> In fact, *reading*, in the sense of consuming, is far from *playing* with the text. "Playing" must be understood here in all its polysemy: the text itself *plays* (like a door, like a machine with "play") and the reader plays twice over, playing the Text as one plays a game, looking for a practice which re-produces it, but, in order that that practice not be reduced to a passive, inner *mimesis* (the Text is precisely that which resists such a reduction), also playing the Text in the musical sense of the term. The history of music (as a practice, not as an "art") does indeed parallel that of the Text fairly closely. (Barthes 1977, 162; italics original)[38]

Barthes would appear to be very close to the idea that the "textual play" indulged in by "active amateurs" also allowed for their participation in the backstage world of the texts' creation. And also to the notion that only after that transitional period between Classicism and Romanticism, with the emergence of professional "interpreters", did their "playing with the text" (1977, 162) begin to occur without their partaking also in the text's creation. Barthes' discussion leads us to believe that "playing with the text" rid itself in this way of its theatrical features and became a strictly intellectual pursuit.

Reading aloud, as a form of the reception of poetry, was a regular pastime in Wirtemberska's salon. It is significant that *Malvina*, a prose work, was also read aloud. This shows that this method of dissemination, which

---

38 It must be said that to Barthes the "text" is equivalent to the "literary text". This means a special, innovative understanding of a literary text as a heterogeneous reality, composed of many texts, which operates within the cultural "intertext". This view of the literary text as "text" defies the view of a literary text as a homogenous and unchanging reality, as a "work".

assumes that the content will be heard, was standard practice not only for poetry but for prose as well. Little is known about the rhetorical and intonational conventions observed by Tadeusz Matuszewicz, a public speaker, performer and politician, as he read *Malvina* aloud to the salon audience. In particular, it is difficult to specify how he distinguished between the sounds of sections of the novel so diverse as the narrator's tale and the protagonists' letters. What we do know is that these readings aloud inspired enormous interest in *Malvina*. What is more, under the influence of these performances, people began to embrace the roles of the novel's characters and to imitate their mannerisms of speech and behaviour. I already discussed all these issues at the beginning of my analysis of the novel. I wished to highlight the fact that before the novel made its way into readers' hands in book form, it had been read aloud in the salon. When embarking on my analysis of *Malvina*, I also focused on the functional, expressive and symbolic separateness of these two modes of its reception. So it is now high time to answer the questions I initially asked concerning the differences between the performance-based and purely readerly reception of the novel. It is also high time to complement my previous conclusions with a few final observations.

Matuszewicz's reading aloud of *Malvina* must have been semantically expressive. He would certainly have used rhetorical and intonational techniques competently. Without them, he would not have been able to impact his listeners so effectively. One can imagine that the declamatory skills of Matuszewicz could have been described with the same phrases used to describe Ludomir's reading aloud of *Ludgarda, a Tragedy*. If echoes of a text by Ludwik Kropiński, a member of Wirtemberska's salon community, can so readily be identified in the text read aloud by Ludomir, why not assume that this mode of reading was practised also by Matuszewicz, likewise a frequenter of Wirtemberska's salon? In one of the novel's episodes, Malvina's sister – Wanda, when writing in a letter about Ludomir's reading-aloud skills, labels them "wonderful" in her very first sentence, and then, in trying to recreate the mood of that moment, uses ambiguous phrases which suggest that Ludomir read "not only with his eyes but with his heart" (24). I have chosen this epistolary account as the motto for this part of my book, so I will not repeat it here. What it shows is that Ludomir (and most probably Matuszewicz as well) read scenes full of sensibility "not only with his eyes but with his heart", while others were rendered – we can imagine – only "with his eyes" (24). We cannot know whether Ludomir (and possibly Matuszewicz too), when reading "not only with his eyes but with his heart", stretched the linguistic rules of intonation to fit vocal or musical models. We cannot know whether, when both readers read "only with the eyes", they approximated the intonation appropriate to common or elevated speech. As a result, it is impossible to determine whether the scenes of sensibility (in Kropiński's *Ludgarda* and in Wirtemberska's *Malvina*) were enhanced with an "inspired" message, while others were read in a "matter-of-fact" manner. This is because we have no way of knowing whether these very labels correspond to what was meant by reading "with the heart" and by reading only "with the eyes". Finally, it cannot be excluded that both readers relied on a whole range of intonational features which extended between the two extremes: the vocal (inspired) and spoken (matter-of-fact).

Although so little is known about the modulations of Matuszewicz's voice and the intentional principles that he observed, we do know that these principles served to qualify semantically the text being read. We also know that the modulation of the reader's voice rendered *Malvina* different from what it became later – as it reached its readers in book form. The techniques used by Matuszewicz made the novel's reception a social activity. Later, the readers' experience of *Malvina* as a book became part of their inner lives.

It was this latter kind of reception of a literary work that Wirtemberska imagined in the preface to her novel – one based on inner "reflections, made without prejudice" (4). The basis for this kind of reception of *Malvina* was the book form, and not a reading aloud – significantly, not only the reading aloud but also the quiet, private reading are portrayed in the novel. In one of the episodes, Malvina tries to pacify her mind through the latter kind of reading.

The listening to *Malvina* imposed a certain way of understanding the novel, not identical with the one later imposed by the book form. In the twentieth century, with its focus on communication studies, it was found that various ways of disseminating literary texts affect the ways in which the texts are understood. Onufry Kopczyński, a language theoretician in Wirtemberska's day, formulated the interdependence of vocal and semantic microstructures as follows: "People create languages and so people have to give them the body of the voice and the soul of the meaning of thoughts" (Kopczyński 1817, 126; trans. M.O.). Interestingly, Barthes talks about the active voice of an utterance as "the grain of the voice" (1975, 66).

We cannot know for sure, but we can assume that in the inner connections between the live voice of Matuszewicz and the written voice of *Malvina* a semantic expression was given to some *quantum* of these subtle relations between the voice and the writing which bring this novel to life. Naturally, only some of these relations – particularly those which determine the shape of the scenes of sensibility – may have been reflected in the salon declamation.

Certainly, Matuszewicz's voice, with its modulated intonation, gave life to both the affective harmonies and discords which run through Malvina's and Ludomir's utterances. In this respect, reading the novel aloud in the salon was more expressive than later individual crystallisations of the novel made by readers. It enabled the sounds of Ludomir's voice and the meanings of his utterances – perceived as conflicted by the protagonist – to come to the fore within real speech phenomena offered by the declaimer. According to Barthes, utterances and "spoken" texts, particularly those governed by affective motivation, are carried in equal measure by "dramatic inflections, subtle stresses, sympathetic accents", and by "the grain of the voice, which is an erotic mixture of timbre and language" (1975, 66). It was this fulfilment of the salon readings of *Malvina* in living, sounding, pulsating speech, which is the natural element of feeling, that gave it remarkable expressive and symbolic force.

Let us remember one thing: in *Malvina*, the connections between the voice and the writing are ubiquitous enough to encompass its entire narrative and event-related material. Yet this can only be received through reading it as a book, and not by listening to it being read aloud. It was this type of read reception that made it possible to trace, on one's own, the diverse elements of the novel's narrative and event-related material. The very fact that Śniadecki chose to review *Malvina* in the epistolary form also shows that he recognised the narrative complexity of the text. It may therefore be assumed that it did not escape other readers. The focus on the relationship between the voice and the writing in *Malvina* was also the foundation of contemporary literary culture, and this should not be underestimated. This foundation was composed, primarily, of conversation and correspondence. For Wirtemberska, these were the aspects of literary culture, original forms of narrative and conveying events, which served as models when she was creating her own novelistic narrative.

Once again, I would like to refer to the questions raised by J. L. Austin, when drawing linguists' attention to the utterance as a speech act – an act in the process of becoming. In order to consider the voice and the intonation from the perspective of these questions, I shall not attempt to present, much less interpret, Austin's theory. I will refer only to some aspects related to elements of the utterance, or – rather – elements of performing an utterance. In the most general terms, I shall touch upon the central aspect of Austin's theory, which is his understanding of an utterance as an illocutionary act, which defines how it ought to be received or understood.

In Austin's theory, in utterances, intonation is an element of a meaning-producing act, and not a phonetic act. It might be repeated, following Rousseau, that it is the tipping point for the production of meaning. It is located on the side of "uttering words", and not "uttering sounds". Austin makes this much clear: "The uttering of noises may be a consequence (physical) of the movement of the vocal organs, the breath, &c.: but the uttering of a word is *not* a consequence of the uttering of a noise, whether physical or otherwise" (1962, 114; italics original). At the same time, he repeats the idea that "the divorce between 'physical' actions and acts of saying something is not in all ways complete – there is some connexion" (Austin 1962, 113). The point is that there is no obstacle, in certain situations – "in some connexions and contexts" (Austin 1962, 113), as he puts it, to subsuming phonetic acts under the illocutionary properties of an utterance. Austin notes and recognises the phenomena which may arise where the phonetic and meaning-producing acts meet, without going into detail. All his effort goes into pinpointing the properties of speech as a meaning-producing act. Austin does not look closely into what would define Malvina's response to the discord between the sound of the voice and the meaning of Ludomir Prince Melsztyński's utterances. In this case, it is more important that Austin's theory enables us to situate phenomena belonging to the phonetic and semantic borderline, related both to the physical (the voice and its sound) and to conventional aspects of phonetic and meaning-producing acts (features of the voice in an utterance), within a whole range of acts that co-create the act of speech. These manifest themselves in human speech as meaningful subcodes, whose origin is located within human mental irrationality and human corporality – as meaningful subcodes of comprehension or influence.

Bibiliography

Aleksandrowicz, Alina. 1974. *"'Błękitne soboty' Wirtemberskiej"* [Wirtemberska's Blue Saturdays] in *Pamiętnik Literacki* 65.3: 3–36.

Aleksandrowicz, Alina. 1978a. *"Polska 'Podróż sentymentalna'"* [*The Polish 'Sentimental Journey'*]. In *Niektóre zdarzenia, myśli i uczucia doznane za granicą* [Certain Events, Thoughts and Feelings Experienced Abroad] by Maria Wirtemberska. Edited by Alina Aleksandrowicz, 5–38. Warsaw: Państwowy Instytut Wydawniczy.

Aleksandrowicz, Alina, ed. 1978b. *Z kręgu Marii Wirtemberskiej. Antologia* [The Circle of Maria Wirtemberska: An Anthology]. Warsaw: Państwowy Instytut Wydawniczy.

Aristotle. N.d. *Rhetoric*. Translated by W. Rhys Roberts. https://ebooks.adelaide.edu.au /a/aristotle/a8rh/index.html

Austin, John Langshaw. 1962. *How to Do Things with Words*. Oxford: Clarendon Press.

Barthes, Roland. 1964. "Éléments de sémiologie". *Communications* 4: 91–135.

Barthes, Roland. 1977. "From Work to Text". In *Image-Music-Text*. Translated by Stephen Heath, 155–164. London: Fontana Press.

Barthes, Roland. 1990. "La Rochefoucauld: 'Reflections or Sentences and Maxims'". In *New Critical Essays*, 3–22. Berkeley: University of California Press.

Barthes, Roland. 1998. *The Pleasure of the Text*. Translated by Richard Miller. New York: Hill and Wang.

Barthes, Roland. 2001. *A Lover's Discourse: Fragments*. Translated by Richard Howard. New York: Hill and Wang.

Bartoszyński, Kazimierz. 1977. *"Sternizm"* [Sterneism]. In *Słownik literatury polskiego Oświecenia* [Dictionary of Polish Enlightenment Literature]. Edited by Teresa Kostkiewiczowa, 678–680. Breslau: Ossolineum.

Bartoszyński, Kazimierz. 1985. "Zagadnienie komunikacji literackiej w utworach narracyjnych" [Literary Communication in Narrative Texts]. In *Teoria i interpretacja* [Theory and Interpretation], 113–146. Warsaw: Państwowy Instytut Wydawniczy.

Billip, Witold. 1978. "Wstęp" [Introduction]. In *Malwina, czyli domyślność serca* [Malvina or the Heart's Intuition] by Maria Wirtemberska, 5–30. Warsaw: Państwowy Instytut Wydawniczy.

Bohomolec, Franciszek. 1967. "O sztuce pisania listów i celujących w niej autorkach" [On the Art of Letter Writing and Outstanding Female Letter Writers]. In *Monitor 1765–1785: Wybór* [Monitor 1765–1785: A Selection]. Edited by Elżbieta Aleksandrowska. Breslau: Ossolineum.

Brodziński, Kazimierz. 1874. "Synonima polskie" [Polish Synonymy]. In *Pisma. Wydanie zupełne, poprawione i dopełnione z nieogłoszonych rękopisów staraniem J. I. Kraszewskiego* [Works. A Complete, Revised and Supplemented Edition with Unpublished Manuscripts by J. I. Kraszewski]. Vol. VII. Posen: J. I. Kraszewski.

Budzyk, Kazimierz. 1946. "Struktura językowa prozy powieściowej" [Language Structure of Novelistic Prose]. In *Stylistyka teoretyczna w Polsce* [Theoretical Stylistics in Poland], 192–207. Łódź: Spółdzielnia Wydawnicza Książka.

Budzyk, Kazimierz. 1966a. "Dwie Malwiny" [Two Malvinas]. In *Prace o literaturze i teatrze ofiarowane Zygmuntowi Szweykowskiemu* [Studies in Literature and Theatre Presented to Zygmunt Szweykowski], 77–90. Breslau: Ossolineum

Budzyk, Kazimierz. 1966b. "Sytuacja 'Malwiny' w powieściopisarstwie polskim" [The Situation of Malvina among Polish Novels]. In *Stylistyka, poetyka, teoria literatury* [Stylistics, Poetics and Literary Theory]. Edited by Hanna Budzykowa and Janusz Sławiński, 145–151. Breslau: Ossolineum.

Burkot, Stanisław. 1968. *Spory o powieść w polskiej krytyce literackiej XIX w.* [Dispute about the Novel in Nineteenth-Century Polish Literary Criticism]. Breslau: Ossolineum.

Derrida, Jacques. 1997. *Of Grammatology: Corrected Edition*. Translated by Gayatri Chakravorty Spivak. Baltimore: Johns Hopkins University Press.

Duchińska, Seweryna. 1886. *Wspomnienia z życia Marii z ks. Czartoryskich ks. Wirtemberskiej*, [Memories of Maria Wirtemberska née Czartoryska]. Warsaw: Drukarnia Nosowskiego.

Florczak, Zofia. 1978. *Europejskie źródła teorii językowych w Polsce na przełomie XVIII i XIX wieku* [European Sources of Polish Theories of Language at the Turn of the Nineteenth Century]. Breslau: Ossolineum.

Foucault, Michel. 2002. *The Order of Things: The Archaelogy of Human Sciences*. London and New York: Routledge.

Genette, Gérard. 1964. "Le serpent dans la bergerie". In *L'Astrée* by Honoré d'Urfé, 7–22. Paris: Union Générale d'Editions.

Genette, Gérard. 1982a. "Frontiers of Narrative". In *Figures of Literary Discourse*. Translated by Alan Sheridan, 127–144. New York: Columbia University Press.

Genette, Gérard. 1982b. "Poetic Language, Poetics of Language". In *Figures of Literary Discourse*. Translated by Alan Sheridan, 75–102. New York: Columbia University Press.

Głowiński, Michał. 1973a. "Dialog w powieści" [Dialogue in the Novel]. In *Gry powieściowe. Szkice z teorii i historii form narracyjnych* [Novelistic Games: Sketches in the Theory and History of Narrative Forms], 37–58. Breslau: Ossolineum.

Głowiński, Michał. 1973b. "Narracja jako monolog wypowiedziany" [Narrative as Spoken Monologue]. In *Gry powieściowe. Szkice z teorii i historii form narracyjnych* [Novelistic Games: Sketches in the Theory and History of Narrative Forms], 106–148. Breslau: Ossolineum.

Głowiński, Michał. 1973c. "O powieści w pierwszej osobie" [On First-Person Novels]. In *Gry powieściowe. Szkice z teorii i historii form narracyjnych* [Novelistic Games: Sketches in the Theory and History of Narrative Forms], 59–75. Breslau: Ossolineum.

Gombrowicz, Witold. 1985. *Cosmos and Pornografia: Two Novels*. Translated by Eric Mosbacher and Alastair Hamilton. New York: Grove Press.

Górny, Wojciech. 1966. "Składnia przytoczenia w języku polskim" [Indirect Speech Syntax in Polish]. In *System składniowo-stylistyczny prozy polskiego renesansu* [The Syntactic and Stylistic System of Polish Renaissance Prose], 281–398. Warsaw: Państwowy Instytut Wydawniczy.

Grajewski, Wincenty. 1977. "Nauka lektury według Rolanda Barthesa" [Learning to Read with Roland Barthes]. In *Problemy odbioru i odbiorcy* [Problems of Reception and Recipients]. Edited by Tadeusz Bujnicki and Janusz Sławiński, 47–56. Breslau: Ossolineum.

Guzek, Andrzej. 1977. "Salony literackie" [Literary Salons]. In *Słownik literatury polskiego Oświecenia* [Dictionary of Polish Enlightenment Literature]. Edited by Teresa Kostkiewiczowa, 633–638. Breslau: Ossolineum.

Herder, Johann Gottfried von. 2004. "Treatise on the Origin of Language". In *Herder: Philosophical Writings*. Translated and edited by Michael N. Forster, 65–164. Cambridge: Cambridge University Press.

Hobson, Marion. 1982. *The Object of Art: The Theory of Illusion in Eighteenth-Century France.* Cambridge: Cambridge University Press.

Hopensztand, Dawid. 1946. "Mowa pozornie zależna w kontekście 'Czarnych skrzydeł'" [Free Indirect Discourse in *Black Wings*]. In *Stylistyka teoretyczna w Polsce* [Theoretical Stylistics in Poland]. Edited by Kazimierz Budzyk, 299–330. Warsaw: Książka.

Ivanov, Vyacheslav V. 1978. *Chet i nechet. Assimetriia mozga i znakovyh system* [Odd and Even: The Asymmetry of the Brain and of the Sign Systems]. Moscow: Sovetskoe Radio.

Ivanov, Vyacheslav V. 1987. "Bliznechnye mify". In *Mify narodov mira. Entsiklopediia.* Vol. 1. Edited by S. A. Tokarev, 174–176. Moscow: Sovetskaia *Entsiklopediia.*

Jones Debska, Anita. 2012. "Sonnet II". In *Migrant Words: Selected Poems by Adam Mickiewicz*, 57. Wivenhoe Press: Wivenhoe, Essex.

Karcevskij, Sergej. 1982. "The Asymmetric Dualism of the Linguistic Sign". In *The Prague School: Selected Writings, 1929–1946*. Translated by Wendy Steiner. Edited by Peter Steiner, 47–54. Austin: University of Texas Press.

Karpiński, Franciszek. 1960. "Rozyno! Gdybyś wiedziała..." [Rosie-Anne, if you but knew...]. *Wiersze wybrane* [Selected Poems], 63–64. *Edited by* Jan Kott. Warsaw: Państwowy Instytut Wydawniczy.

Kleiner, Juliusz. *1981.* "Powieść Marii z Czartoryskich ks. Wirtemberskiej" [Princess Maria Wirtemberska née Czartoryska's Novel]. In *Juliusz Kleiner. W kręgu historii i teorii literatury* [Juliusz Kleiner: on the History and Theory of Literature]. Edited by Artur Hutnikiewicz, 157–174. Warsaw: Państwowe Wydawnictwo Naukowe.

Kloch, Zbigniew. 1993. "O słownikach synonimów z początku XIX wieku" [On Early Nineteenth-Century Thesauruses]. *Teksty Drugie* 2: 43–56.

Kopczyński, Onufry. 1817. *Gramatyka języka polskiego* [Polish Grammar]. Warsaw: Drukarnia XX Pijarów.

Kostkiewiczowa, Teresa. 1964. *Model liryki sentymentalnej w twórczości Franciszka Karpińskiego* [The Model of the Sentimental Lyric in Franciszek Karpiński's Poetry]. Breslau: Ossolineum.

Kostkiewiczowa, Teresa. 1990. "'Przewodnik słów polskich do prawdy'. O poglądach ludzi Oświecenia na zjawisko manipulacji językowej" [A Guide of Polish Vocabulary to Truth: Enlightenment Views on Language Manipulation]. *Pamiętnik Literacki* 81.3: 145–162.

Krasicki, Ignacy. 1992. *The Adventures of Mr. Nicholas Wisdom.* Evanston: Northwestern University Press.

Kremer-Marietti, Angèle. 1974. "Jean-Jacques Rousseau ou la double origine et son rapport au système langue – musique – politique". In *Essai sur l'origine des langues*, by Jean-Jacques Rousseau, 1–83. Paris: Aubier Montaigne.

Lacan, Jacques. 1991. "Sosie". In *The Seminar of Jacques Lacan. Book II. The Ego in Freud's Theory and in the Technique of Psychoanalysis 1954–1955.* Translated by Sylvana Tomaselli. Edited by Jacques-Alain Miller, 259–275. New York and London: W. W. Norton.

Lathuillère, Roger. 1966. *La Préciosité. Étude historique et linguistique*. Vol. 1. Genève: Droz.

Leibniz, Gottfried Wilhelm. 1996. *New Essays on Human Understanding*. Translated and edited by Peter Remnant and Jonathan Bennett. Cambridge: Cambridge University Press.

Libera, Zdzisław. 1982. "Le problème de l'illustration dans le roman sentimental polonais au début du XIX siècle". In *L'illustration du livre et la littérature au XVIII siècle en France et en Pologne*, 289–303. Warsaw: Éditions de l'Université de Varsovie.

Lipiński, Jacek. 1955. "Aktor i scena w recenzjach teatralnych Towarzystwa Iksów" [Actors and the Stage in Theatre Reviews by the X Society]. *Pamiętnik Teatralny* 14.2: 101–132.

Lotman, Yu. M. 1992. "'Ezda v ostrov liubvi' Trediakovskogo i funktsiia perevodnoi literatury v russkoi kul'ture pervoi poloviny XVIII v." In *Izbrannye stat'i*. Vol. 2. Tallinn: Aleksandra.

Lotman, Yu. M., and B. A. Uspensky. 1978. "Myth – Name – Culture". *Semiotica* 22.3–4: 211–233.

Lyons, John. 1977. *Semantics*. Vol. 1. Cambridge: Cambridge University Press.

Mayenowa, Maria Renata. 1970. "Teoria języka i poezji na terenie romańskim. G. Vico i J. J. Rousseau" [The Theory of Language and Poetry in Romanesque Lands: Vico and Rousseau]. In *Język i poezja. Z dziejów świadomości XVIII wieku*. [Language and Poetry: from the History of Eighteenth-Century Consciousness]. Edited by Janusz Sławiński, Teresa Kostkiewiczowa and Jan Trzynadlowski, 9–24. Breslau: Ossolineum.

Mickiewicz, Adam. 2002. "To M***". In *Polish Romantic Literature: An Anthology*. Translated by Michael J. Mikoś, 28–29. Bloomington, Indiana: Slavica Publishers.

Molière. 1904. *Amphitryon*. Project Gutenberg. Translated by A. R. Waller. http://www .archive.org/stream/amphitryon02536gut/amphi10.txt

Okopień-Sławińska, Aleksandra. 1985. "Semantyka relacji osobowych" [The Semantics of Personal Relations]. In *Semantyka wypowiedzi poetyckiej. Preliminaria* [The Semantics of Poetical Utterance: Fundamentals], 57–116. Breslau: Ossolineum.

Okopień-Sławińska, Aleksandra. 1988. "Retoryka" [Rhetoric]. In *Słownik terminów literackich* [Dictionary of Literary Terms], 433. Breslau: Ossolineum.

Osiński, Ludwik. 1862. "Deklamacya" ["Recitation"]. In *Dzieła* [Works]. Vol. IV. Warsaw: Drukarnia Jaworskiego.

Picard, Roger. 1966. *Les salons littéraires et la société français, 1670–1739*. New York: Brentano's.

Plato. 2008. *The Symposium*. Translated by M. C. Howatson. Edited by M. C. Howatson and Frisbee C. C. Sheffield. Cambridge: Cambridge University Press.

Redfield, James M. 1994. *Nature and Culture in the Iliad: The Tragedy of Hector*. Durham and London: Duke University Press.

Ricoeur, Paul. 1984–1985. *Time and Narrative*. 2 vols. Translated by Kathleen McLaughlin and David Pellauer. Chicago: University of Chicago Press.

Ricoeur, Paul. 1985. "The Metamorphoses of the Plot". In *Time and Narrative*. Vol. 2. Translated by Kathleen McLaughlin and David Pellauer, 7–28. Chicago: University of Chicago Press.

Rousseau, Jean-Jacques. 1979. *Émile or On Education*. Translated by Allan Bloom. New York: Basic Books.

Rousseau, Jean-Jacques. 1998. *Essay on the Origin of Languages and Writings Related to Music*. Translated and edited by John T. Scott. Hanover, NH: University Press of New England.

Sapir, Edward. 1973. "Speech as Personality Trait". In *Selected Writing of Edward Sapir on Language, Culture and Personality*. Edited by David G. Mandelbaum, 533–543. Berkeley: University of California Press.

Schefer, Jean-Louis. 1969. *Scénographie d'un tableau*. Paris: Éditions du Seuil.

Shklovsky, Viktor. 1923. "Evgenii Onegin". In *Ocherki po poetike Pushkina*, 199–220. Berlin: Epocha.

Shklovsky, Viktor. 1964. "Angliiskii klassicheskii roman". In *Khudozhestvennaia proza: razmyshleniia i razbory*. Polish translation by Seweryn Pollak: "Angielska powieść klasyczna" [Classic English Novel]. *O prozie. Rozważania i analizy* [Prose: Studies and Analyses], 7–184. Vol. 2. Warsaw: Państwowy Instytut Wydawniczy.

Shklovsky, Viktor. 1991. *Theory of Prose*. Translated by Benjamin Sher. Elmwood Park, IL: Dalkey Archive Press.

Shklovsky, Viktor. 1991. "The Novel as Parody: Sterne's *Tristram Shandy*". In *Theory of Prose*. Translated by Benjamin Sher, 141–170. Elmwood Park, IL: Dalkey Archive Press.

Sikora, Jan. 1970. "Język, myślenie, uczucie w twórczości J. G. Herdera" [Language, Thinking and Feeling in Herder's Oeuvre]. In *Język i poezja. Z dziejów świadomości XVIII wieku*. [Language and Poetry: from the History of Eighteenth-Century Consciousness]. Edited by Janusz Sławiński, Teresa Kostkiewiczowa and Jan Trzynadlowski, 49–69. Breslau: Ossolineum.

Sławiński, Janusz. 1975. "Jedno z poruszeń w przedmiocie" [A Contribution]. *Teksty: teoria literatury, krytyka, interpretacja* 22.4: 1–5.

Słowacki, Euzebiusz. 1826. "Rodzaje wymowy w mowie niewiązanej" [Types of Rhetoric in Prose]. In *Dzieła* [Works]. Vol. II. Vilnius: Józef Zawadzki.

Słowacki, Juliusz. 1944. *"In Switzerland"*. In *A Polish Anthology*. Translated by M. A. Michael. Edited by T. M. Filip, 231–255. London: Duckworth.

Sterne, Lawrence. 2005. *The Life and Opinions of Tristram Shandy, Gentleman; A Sentimental Journey through France and Italy*. Munich: Günter Jürgensmeier.

Śniadecki, Jan. 2003. "'Malwina': List stryja do synowicy, pisany z Warszawy 31 stycznia 1816 roku z przesłaniem nowego romansu" [An Uncle's Epistle to his Niece, Written from Warsaw on 31 January 1816, on Sending her a New Romance]. In *Jan Śniadecki: Wybór pism estetyczno-literackich* [Jan Śniadecki: Selected Works in Aesthetics and Literature], 22–33. Krakow: Universitas.

Tokarev, S. A. 1987. "Dvupolye sushhestva". In *Mify narodov mira. Entsiklopediia*. Vol. 1. Edited by S. A. Tokarev, 358–359. Moscow: Sovetskaia *Entsiklopediia*.

Watt, Ian. 1965. *The Rise of the Novel: Studies in Defoe, Richardson and Fielding*. Berkeley: University of California Press.

Wirtemberska, Maria. 2012. *Malvina, or the Heart's Intuition*. Trans. Ursula Phillips. DeKalb, IL: NIU Press.

Wirtemberska, Maria. 1978 [1816–1818]. *Niektóre zdarzenia, myśli i uczucia doznane za granicą* [Certain Events, Thoughts and Feelings Experienced Abroad]. Edited by Alina Aleksandrowicz. Warsaw: Państwowy Instytut Wydawniczy.

Witkowska, Alina. 1971. "Wstęp" [Introduction]. In *Polski romans sentymentalny* [Polish Sentimental Romance], iii–lxxxv. Breslau: Ossolineum.

Wittgenstein, Ludwig. 1993. "Lecture on Ethics". In *Philosophical Occasions*. Edited by James Klage and Alfred Nordman, 36–44. Indianapolis: Hackett Publishing.

Zabłocki, Franciszek. 1829 [1783]. "Amfitrio. Komedya we trzech aktach z Moliera" [Amphitryon: A Three-Act Comedy after Molière]. In *Dzieła* [Works]. Vol. 6. Warsaw: F. S. Dmochowski.